Humpty Dumpty

A Pantomime

Book by John Crocker
Lyrics by Eric Gilder

Samuel French - London
New York - Sydney - Toronto - Hollywood

Copyright © 1975 John Crocker and Eric Gilder
All Rights Reserved

HUMPTY DUMPTY is fully protected under the copyright laws of the British Commonwealth, including Canada, the United States of America, and all other countries of the Copyright Union. All rights, including professional and amateur stage productions, recitation, lecturing, public reading, motion picture, radio broadcasting, television and the rights of translation into foreign languages are strictly reserved.

ISBN 978-0-573-16413-2

www.samuelfrench.co.uk
www.samuelfrench.com

FOR AMATEUR PRODUCTION ENQUIRIES

UNITED KINGDOM AND WORLD
EXCLUDING NORTH AMERICA

plays@samuelfrench.co.uk

020 7255 4302/01

Each title is subject to availability from Samuel French, depending upon country of performance.

CAUTION: Professional and amateur producers are hereby warned that HUMPTY DUMPTY is subject to a licensing fee. Publication of this play does not imply availability for performance. Both amateurs and professionals considering a production are strongly advised to apply to the appropriate agent before starting rehearsals, advertising, or booking a theatre. A licensing fee must be paid whether the title is presented for charity or gain and whether or not admission is charged.

The Professional Rights in this play are controlled by Samuel French Ltd, 24-32 Stephenson Way, London NW1 2HD.

No one shall make any changes in this title for the purpose of production. No part of this book may be reproduced, stored in a retrieval system, or transmitted in any form, by any means, now known or yet to be invented, including mechanical, electronic, photocopying, recording, videotaping, or otherwise, without the prior written permission of the publisher. No one shall upload this title, or part of this title, to any social media websites.

The right of John Crocker and Eric Gilder to be identified as author of this work has been asserted in accordance with Section 77 of the Copyright, Designs and Patents Act 1988.

PRODUCTION NOTE

Pantomime, as we know it today, is a form of entertainment all on its own, derived from a number of different sources – the commedia dell'arte (and all that that derived from), the ballet, opera, music hall and the realms of folklore and fairy tale. And elements of all of these are still to be found in it. This strange mixture has created a splendid topsy-turvy world where men are women, women are men, where the present is embraced within the past, where people are hit but not hurt, where authority is constantly flouted, where everything is open to ridicule including pantomime itself at times and, above all, where magic abounds and dreams invariably come true. In other words, it is – or should be – fun. Fun to do and fun to watch and the sense of enjoyment which can be conveyed by a cast is very important to the enjoyment of the audience.

Pantomime can be very simply staged if resources are limited. Basically a tab surround at the back, tab legs at the sides and a set of traverse tabs for the frontcloth scenes, together with the simplest of cut-out pieces to suggest the various locales, (or even just placards with this information written on them), will suffice. Conversely, there is no limit to the extent to which more lavish facilities can be employed.

The directions I have given in the text adopt a middle course and are based on a permanent setting of a cyclorama sky-cloth at the back and, about two thirds of the depth downstage, a false proscenium, immediately behind which are the lines for a set of traverse tabs. Below the false proscenium are arched entrances left and right with reveals if necessary to the proscenium. A border will be required at some point between the false proscenium and the cyclorama to mask lighting battens and the top of the cyclorama. Lastly, there are sets of steps leading down into the auditorium at both the front corners of the stage.

Into this permanent setting are placed cut-out backings and various wings left and right. The frontcloth fly lines come in behind the traverse tabs. Cloths can, of course, be tumbled or rolled if flying space is limited. I have indicated that the traverse tabs should be closed for the beginning of most frontcloth scenes, then if any hitch occurs while flying in the cloth the lights can still come up and the actors get on with the scene. Similarly, I have, where possible, given cues before the ends of these scenes for the tabs to be closed again to allow time for the cloths to be flown out. Thus, each scene can flow swiftly into the next, an important point if a smooth-running production is to be achieved.

The settings and costumes should preferably be in clear bright colours to give a story-book effect. I think it best to have everything in one period – apart from deliberate anachronisms in some of the comics' costumes – but which period is immaterial. HUMPTY's first costume should preferably be in yellow and white to reflect his association with the Egg. Animal skins for the horses can be hired from Barnum's Carnival Novelties, 67 Hammersmith Road, London, W.14 or from Theatre Zoo, 28 New Row, London, W.C.2.

The special lighting equipment I have indicated – a Strobe Freeze Light between Scenes 1 and 2, Snow and Rain Lanterns in Scene 4 and a Harlequin Strobe Lantern in Scene 5 – can be hired from the usual stage electrical suppliers, as can flash boxes and powder. The special lanterns are not absolute necessities, but they are impressive if resources permit. I have not attempted to give a complete lighting plot as this entirely depends on the equipment available, but generally speaking most pantomime lighting should be full-up, warm and bright. Pinks and ambers are probably best for this and a circuit of blues in the cyclorama battens for the dawn-rise, night falling and any other dramatic effects. Follow spots are a great help, but not essential. If they are available it is often effective in romantic numbers to fade out the stage lighting and hold the principals in the follow spots, quickly fading up the full lighting on the last few bars because this can help to increase the applause!

Pantomime needs many props and often they will have to be home-made. Any of the more awkward seeming ones are dealt with in 'Special Instructions'. Props should be colourfully painted and in pantomime many of them should be larger than reality. It is also wise for the property master to examine carefully the practical use to which a prop is to be put; a whole comedy sequence often depends on something working properly.

The music has been specially composed so that it is easy for the less musically accomplished to master, but it is also scored in parts for the more musically ambitious. If an orchestra is available well and good, but a single piano will suffice. It is an advantage, however, if there can be a drummer as well; not only because a rhythm accompaniment enhances the numbers, but also because, for some reason never yet fully fathomed, slapstick hits and falls seem twice as funny if they coincide with a well-timed bonk on a drum, wood-block or whatever is found to make the noise best suited to the action. If necessary, though, some of the effects, such as the Swanee whistle ones, can be done off-stage.

Pantomime demands a particular style of playing and production. The acting must be larger than life, but still sincere, with a good deal of sparkle and attack. Much of it must be projected directly at the audience, since one of pantomime's great advantages is that it deliberately breaks down the 'fourth wall'. The actors can literally and metaphorically shake hands with their audience who become almost memberts of the cast; indeed, their active participation from time to time is essential. A word of warning on this, though - the actors must always remain in control; they must never encourage a response to such an extent that they can no longer be heard. This is particularly so in the case of hissing, which I think FOWLPEST should discourage. If his every appearance is drowned in a sea of hisses much of the effect of his part, and much of the plot too, will be lost. And the plot of a pantomime is of prime importance because the larger part of the audience, the children, like stories and like to be able to follow them. Therefore, the producer should ensure that the story line is clearly brought out. This is especially important in 'Humpty Dumpty' which has no well-known story. The plot I have evolved from the few details given in the nursery rhyme is purposely complicated and its very intricacy should be put over as a kind of joke by the cast. However, it is not so involved that it is beyond the comprehension of children - the adults might find it a bit tricky but their juniors will be able to explain it to them.

Teamwork is very necessary in pantomime; every member of the cast should allow whoever has the important bit in a scene to be the focus of attention. The selfish actor continually hogging the limelight is distracting to the audience and very aggravating to the rest of the cast! There is always room for local gags and topical quips in pantomime, but they should not be overdone. Nor should any of the comedy - too much 'milking' or too long dwelling on something the cast think is hilarious but obviously the audience does not can slow down the pace disastrously, and much of this script should go at a pretty spanking pace. It should also be appreciated that any comedy scene needs rhythm and a shape; a big laugh in the wrong place can upset the balance and actually make the sequence as a whole less funny. Last, but certainly not least, the comedy must never appear to be conscious of its own funniness.

Characterization should be clear and definite. I prefer the traditional use of a man to play the Dame and a girl to play the Principal Boy. In the case of the Dame, anyway, there is a sound argument for this; audiences will laugh more readily at a man impersonating a woman involved in the mock cruelties of slapstick than at a real woman. For this reason an actor playing a Dame should never quite let us forget he is a man, while giving a sincere character performance of a woman; further, he can be as feminine as he likes but never effeminate. HETTY HENCAKE is a high-spirited, good-hearted soul. There must be nothing suggestive in her lively interest in men – it reflects her optimism more than anything else.

Like the Dame a Principal Boy also requires a character performance, but with the implications reversed, of course! An occasional slap of the thigh is not enough. ROMANO should preferably be dark and certainly romantic-looking and if this quality can be leavened with a touch of humour so much the better.

Principal Girls can be a bore, but only if they are presented as mere pretty symbols of feminine sweetness. Obviously PRINCESS EGLANTINE should be pretty, but she also has a sense of fun and is not lacking in toughness and determination when it is required.

HUMPTY DUMPTY should be ovoid in shape, either naturally or with the help of some padding. He has a whimsical outlook on life and is not a forceful individual; he accepts whatever comes along and accepts it with a good grace.

CHICKWEED is ingenuous, eager, enthusiastic and wholehearted in whatever she does. Her loyalty to her master, MR FOWLPEST, is total until she meets HUMPTY and then her devotion to him is overwhelming. The actress playing her will have ample opportunities to display her comic talents.

The actor playing FOWLPEST will have similar opportunities. The WIZARD has a higher opinion of his abilities than his achievements warrant and his volatile temperament switches from baffled rage to complacent self-congratulation with remarkable rapidity. A great deal of the motivation of the story depends on him, though, so he must not be without weight and authority.

His opponent, ALBUMENIA, is not lacking in such qualities either. She is a down-to-earth, no-nonsense type, but very jolly with it, rather like a benevolent hockey mistress.

KING ADDLEPATE is vague and affable but he does know how to use a little regal dignity when the situation requires it.

SERGEANT RANK tries to be the epitome of bustling efficiency, but with PRIVATE FILE for a subordinate his efforts are usually doomed to failure in spite of FILE's abundant willingness, not that FILE himself is at all dismayed by his shortcomings.

The actor playing UNDERDOWN can enjoy himself being incredibly old, but he must also bring out the antipodean undertones of the part to realise the comedy fully.

DOT is a more skittish and mischievous horse than her stable companion, CARRYONE, who has a more lumbering approach to life.

I have made provision for a CHORUS of ten, but naturally the number used will depend on how many are available.

JOHN CROCKER

CHARACTERS

HUMPTY DUMPTY		
ADDLEPATE THE DOZENTH	-	King of Goldova
PRINCESS EGLANTINE	-	His Daughter
SERGEANT RANK)		
PRIVATE FILE)	-	The King's Men
DOT)		
CARRYONE)	-	The King's Horses
HETTY HENCAKE	-	The Chief Chicken-Maid
ROMANO	-	A Gipsy
ALBUMENIA	-	The White Witch
FOWLPEST	-	The Wicked Wizard
CHICKWEED	-	His Witchlet Apprentice
UNDERDOWN	-	King of the Goblins

Chorus as - A ROOSTER, HENS, CHICKEN-MAIDS, SOLDIERS, HARLEQUIN, RAINBOW SPIRITS, GIPSIES and GOBLINS

SYNOPSIS OF SCENES

PART I

Scene 1	The Palace Wall
Scene 2	The Wizard's Den
Scene 3	The Royal Cavalry Stables
Scene 4	On The Way To Somewhere
Scene 5	The End of the Rainbow

PART II

Scene 6	The Gipsy Camp
Scene 7	Outside the Palace
Scene 8	The Haunted Bedroom
Scene 9	On The Way To The Way Down
Scene 10	Goblin Land
Scene 11	Sheer Magic
Scene 12	The Palace Throne Room

HUMPTY DUMPTY

MUSIC 1 OVATURE

PART ONE

Scene One : The Palace Wall

Across the back of the stage is a wall with a cut-out glimpse of the Palace beyond. C. on the wall is a large Egg, and below it a notice:
'If this Egg should tumble down
Addlepate will lose his crown.'
At R. is a housepiece with a practical door fitted with a knocker, bell-pull and letter-box. On one side of the door is a window covered by shutters, and on the other a plate inscribed 'ALBUMENIA, WHITE WITCH, BY APPOINTMENT TO THE KING OF GOLDOVA' over a coat of arms, which is a gold egg surmounted by a crown and supported by two heraldic hens on a white field. At L. is an Inn piece with practical door. A sign hangs out - 'YE OLDE SPANISH OMELETTE'. Outside the Inn is a trick tub table. A shelf has been fixed at about shoulder height L. on the false proscenium.

MUSIC 2 DOING IT ON THE CHEEP

The music starts softly and the Cyc., is streaked with the light of early dawn. Two of the CHORUS as SOLDIERS are discovered leaning against the wall below the Egg, dozing. A ROOSTER (one of the CHORUS) struts on, on the wall if possible, lifts his head and crows. The music echoes his call. The SOLDIERS are startled awake, but see that all is well with the Egg and stretch themselves. LIGHTS start to FADE UP and the music builds. ROOSTER crows again and this time is answered by the clucking of some hens. This is provided by some of the CHORUS as three HENS. The remainder of the CHORUS enter with them as two CHICKEN-MAIDS and two more SOLDIERS, who are their escort party. The Opening Chorus proceeds with the SOLDIERS vying for the CHICKEN-MAIDS, while the ROOSTER jumps down from the wall to impress his own females.

SOLDIERS & CHICKEN-MAIDS	Don't waste the morning lazily playing, You lay-abouts, get on with your laying. Orders is orders, so do as you're told And lay us some eggs of gold.
HENS	Puk - puk - puk - puk, er - er.
ROOSTER	Cock-a-doodle-doo!
	(The ROOSTER chases the HENS off R., while the 1st and 2nd SOLDIERS plant a kiss on either cheek of the 1st CHICKEN-MAID and the 3rd and 4th SOLDIERS deal similarly with the 2nd CHICKEN-MAID.
	MUSIC 3
	SERGEANT RANK, a brisk little man, marches smartly on from L. and stops in outraged astonishment.)
RANK	What's going on 'ere?
	(The SOLDIERS spring guiltily away and stand to attention. CHICKEN-MAIDS laugh and run R.)
	You 'orrible little men! And you come back 'ere, you 'orrible little chicken-maids!
1st C.M.	No fear!
2nd C.M.	We're not in the army.
1st C.M.) 2nd C.M.)	You 'orrible little man!
	(They laugh and run off R. DRUMMERS and SOLDIERS smother a laugh. RANK wheels round on them.)
RANK	You didn't 'ear that! Talking to me like that - me, Sergeant Rank! I shall report them to the chief Chicken-Maid, Miss 'Etty 'Encake. (To Audience.) Note that name, you'll be meeting 'er later. (To others.) So, now I know what's going on 'ere. There's goings-on going on. Yes, goings-on going on behind my back. And what's worse, goings-on going on behind my back in front of my very eyes! A fine way to carry out your duties.
1st SOLDIER	But, Sarge, we were only guarding the Egg.

HUMPTY DUMPTY 3

3rd SOLDIER	And we were only escorting the Royal Hen Party.
RANK	Only! Just you listen to me. (To Audience.) And you lot listen carefully, too. This is an IMPORTANT BIT. (To 1st and 2nd SOLDIERS.) That there hegg 'as been up there for twenty years and so's that there warning. So why are you guarding the Hegg?
1st SOLDIER	So that it doesn't tumble down.
RANK	'Cos what 'appens if it does?
2nd SOLDIER	The King loses his crown.
RANK	Correct. (To 3rd and 4th SOLDIERS.) And as for you two, as hescort to the Royal 'En Party you wasn't only looking after a few 'ens, you was looking after the country's 'ole heconomy. 'Cos why?
1st SOLDIER	'Cos they're special hens.
RANK	And what's special about them?
2nd SOLDIER	They lay gold eggs.
RANK	Eggactly! (Looks at them.) I said, <u>egg</u>actly. (Gets no reaction from them.) Wake up! That was a touch of humour to lighten a serious moment. Eggactly, laughing by numbers – one!
1st SOLDIER	Ha-ha!
RANK	Two!
2nd SOLDIER	Ha-ha!
RANK	Three!
3rd SOLDIER	Ha-ha!
RANK	Four!
4th SOLDIER	Ha-ha!
RANK	(to Audience) Five! Ah, some of you not paying attention properly. Back to the serious moment. (To SOLDIERS.) With you looking after them valuable birds the country could go broke; yes, broke, our glorious Goldova! Where are them 'ens

now I ask? And what can you reply?

(HENS run on R. chased by ROOSTER.)

1st SOLDIER They're behind you, Sarge.

RANK Eh?

(HENS and ROOSTER run across and off L. CHICKEN-MAIDS run across after them.)

Well, don't just stand there! Quick, after them birds!

SOLDIERS Yes, Sarge!

(SOLDIERS run eagerly off L.)

RANK (calling after them) Oi! I mean the feathered ones. Now there's nobody to guard the Hegg. (Sighs.) I shall just 'ave to call up the rest of the harmy. (Calling to off L.) Private File! Private File!

MUSIC 4

(PRIVATE FILE, a large untidy-looking soldier, marches on backwards R. bearing a rifle at the slope. A mirror set in the wings will enable him to march in a straight line.)

Private –

(FILE bumps into him and marks time with one foot only.)

FILE Hullo-o!

RANK Hullo? (Moving round to face him.) What do you mean by marching on 'ere backwards?

FILE Well, I was facing that way when you called me.

RANK Facing that way?! And stop waggling your foot about.

FILE I'm not waggling my foot about. I'm marking time.

RANK But you're supposed to use both feet to mark time.

FILE Ooh, I don't like using both feet.

RANK Why not?

FILE I fall over. (Lifts other foot at same time and

HUMPTY DUMPTY

falls.) See?

RANK (controls himself and turns to Audience) This is not an important bit.

FILE It's quite an important bit to me. (Rises rubbing behind tenderly.) Ooh, yes, poor little -

RANK Oh, blow your pool little -

FILE Blow it? Will that make it better? (Tries to.) I don't think I can.

RANK I didn't mean I wanted you to blow it, I meant -

FILE You were going to blow it for me? How kind. (Bends over towards him.)

RANK Certainly not! Stand to attention like a proper soldier.

(FILE does his best with his rifle at the slope (i.e. on L. shoulder). During the following he gradually leans over to his L.)

Now, pay careful attention. Due to a hunfortunate series of circumstances I am forced to - What's the matter now?

FILE It's this rifle. It gets so heavy.

RANK Ho, very well. I'll stand you at ease then. Private File - order - arms!

FILE Order arms? Oh. Well, I'll have a pistol, a cannon and two penn'orth of cannon balls.

RANK No, no! <u>Order arms!</u> Like this. (Demonstrates, using his swagger stick.) Down! Two-three. Over! Two-three. Cut!

(The movements of odering arms from the slope are:
1. 'Down'. The L. arm holding the rifle is straightened which slides the rifle down vertically by the L. side; at the same time the R. arm is bent smartly across the chest to slap the R. hand on the barrel in front of the L. shoulder.
2. 'Over'. The R. hand grasps the barrel and moves the rifle across the body to the R. side with the butt almost resting on the ground, while the L. hand moves over to steady the weapon with the fingers on the muzzle.

	3. 'Cut'. The butt is banged to the ground and the L. hand is cut smartly to the L. side.)
FILE	Oh, you did do that well. I bet I don't. Let's see, what was it? Er – Down! (Executes first movement and in doing so slaps himself on L. shoulder harder than he would have wished.) Ooh! I'm glad I don't do this often. I say, I've just remembered, the last time I did the next bit I had a nasty accident.
RANK	(stepping in to FILE's R.) Ho! And what was that?
FILE	Well, I went – Over! and – (Executes second movement landing his rifle butt on RANK's foot.)
RANK	Wow!
FILE	That was it.
RANK	You blithering idiot! That was my foot!
FILE	I know. It was the same foot last time. Why don't you put the other foot there next time.
RANK	Next time! Listen, you 'orrible little man –
FILE	What? Where? Who came on?
RANK	Hi mean you!
FILE	Me? But I'm much bigger than you are. (Feels top of head.) Or have I shrunk?
RANK	No, you 'aven't, you great – lanky length of longth. Of course, you would be the only one wot I got left to guard the Hegg.
FILE	(pleased) Guard the Egg? Me?
RANK	Yes, and I mean guard it, not see 'ow quick you can knock it down. Is your rifle loaded?
FILE	Ah! Sort of. It's rather fun really. Look. (Raises rifle and points it at RANK.)
RANK	(hastily retreating U.S.) Hey! Don't point it at me!
FILE	(moving up level with him) It's all right, I'm only going to press the trigger.

HUMPTY DUMPTY

(Presses trigger. A little flag with the word 'BANG' on it drops down at the end of the barrel. RANK gives a startled cry and flings up his arms and knocks the Egg with his swagger stick. It begins to rock from side to side.)

RANK Hey! The Hegg! Do something! Stop it!

(They start to run to and fro with the motion of the Egg.)

It's going your way! No, my way! No, your way!

(They collide and fall. As they rise, with the Egg slowing down and stopping, the HENS run on L. clucking loudly followed by the ROOSTER crowing equally loudly. He chases them in a circle round RANK and FILE, who argue ad lib as to whose fault it was that the Egg was knocked. The livestock are shortly followed by the CHICKEN-MAIDS and they by the SOLDIERS: all of whom add to the clamour by cheeping and calling to the HENS.

MUSIC 5

PRINCESS EGLANTINE enters R., dressed for riding.)

PRINCESS Hullo - Good morning - I say -

(Nobody pays any attention to her. She sighs and turns to the Audience.)

Well, obviously I'm not an important bit, even if I am the Princess.

(The HENS and ROOSTER stream past her to run off R. The CHICKEN-MAIDS following them suddenly see the PRINCESS and stop with a hasty curtsey.)

CHICKEN-MAIDS Your Highness!

(SOLDIERS, close behind them, also stop and stand at attention.)

SOLDIERS The Princess!

(FILE sees her and tries to point her out to RANK.)

RANK You flea-brained, jumped-up, never-come-down, boggle-eyed son of a blue-nosed, blue-faced, blue-

PRINCESS	(tapping him on shoulder) Sergeant.
RANK	Go away! – baboon, you are a public danger to me, to the army, the the King, even to –
PRINCESS	Excuse me –
RANK	I don't care who you are, go away! Where did I get to? Oh, yes, even to our lovely little Princess.
PRINCESS	But I am your lovely little Princess.
RANK	(mocking her tones and turning slowly) Ho, so you are our lovely little Princess, are you? – Yes, you are! (Stamps rigidly to attention.) Private File, Royal salute, present – arms!
FILE	Oh yes, what a relief. (Offering rifle to PRINCESS with a deep curtsey.) There!
RANK	No, no, no!
PRINCESS	(intervening hastily) Sergeant, Father and I would like to go for our ride soon.
RANK	Of course, ma'am. Leave it to us, ma'am. 'Is Majesty and you shall 'ave the finest pair of 'orses in the Cavalry Stables.
PRINCESS	I'm sure we shall, because after all there are only two horses in the Cavalry Stables.
RANK	Eh? Oh yes. Private File, left turn! (RANK turns L. but FILE turns R. so that they come face to face.) The other left, fool! (FILE about turns.) Quick – march! (FILE steps backwards as RANK moves forward.) Forwards! (Pushes him and they exit L. PRINCESS laughs and CHORUS join in with her.)
PRINCESS	I see nothing's changed much today. The hens have got loose, that Rooster's always more than loose and Rank and File have had their usual friendly morning

chat. In fact, life's becoming, well -

MUSIC 6   MONOTONOUS

Monotonous -
My life is always so monotonous.
There isn't anything as rotten as
   The yawning in the morning, whereas
I'd rather far make hay in the daytime,
Doing my nut to give me a gay time,
Singing a song and laughing to show that
   I would do anything, long as it isn't

Monotonous;
But all around me it's monotonous.
The circumstances are a blot on us -
   The snoring is so boring, whereas
I want to do some dancing that wiggles;
I want to have a fit of the giggles,
Throwing my bonnet over the windmill -
   Happy things, snappy things, lazy things, crazy
                                                                   things.

Give me just a moonbeam to walk with,
   And pennies jumping out of my purse.
Give me some nice people to talk with,
   And all things that are just the reverse
Of

Monotonous.
I've used the word before - monotonous.
Where have the wheels of progress gotten us?
   I'm thinking that it's stinking, whereas
I want to live a life that's exciting,
Find me a man who's really inviting,
I'll blow my top, and prove that life's not
Monotonous, monotonous, monotonous.

(CHORUS exit.)

Perhaps something exciting will happen soon. Why, the very next person I meet could be the most romantic, glamorous, good-looking -

MUSIC 7

(KING ADDLEPATE wanders in vaguely L., also dressed for riding, but with partricularly wide breeches and wearing a bowler hat with his crown perched on top of it. On his feet, though, he has only a pair of carpet slippers of which the L. one is fitted with a large spur. He is shaking his head over an imposing looking letter and gives EGLANTINE only a perfunctory glance.)

KING — Morning.

PRINCESS — Well, the next person but one maybe. Morning, Daddy.

KING — Daddy? That rings a bell. Oh, yes, it's me, isn't it? Really, my memory, I'll forget me own name next. I have! No, no, it's - er -

PRINCESS — Addlepate.

KING — Of course! Addlepate the Dozenth. And you're - er -

PRINCESS — Eglantine.

KING — Yes! My little half-dozenth. I mean, my little daughter. And I'm all ready for our ride, you see. (Holding up R. foot.) All booted and - (Realises slipper.) carpet boots?

PRINCESS — (laughing) Oh, Daddy dearest, you say that every morning. I don't believe you've got any riding boots.

KING — Oh yes, I have. Definitely. They've got spurs on. I wouldn't wear spurs on slippers, would I?

PRINCESS — (looking at his L. foot) Well -

KING — No, they'd get in the way when I do my morning exercises. (Does a knees-bend and lands on the spur.) Ow! I've just remembered - that's why I gave up doing exercises. Now what's this? Oh, yes. Very worrying. It's a letter from Underdown, The King of the Goblins. He's threatening to over-run -

PRINCESS — (overlapping) - to overrun the Kingdom with his Goblin multitudes unless you give him my hand in marriage.

KING — Precisely, but how did you guess?

PRINCESS	Because he always does, regularly, every three months.
KING	By Jove, yes. I remember now. Er - what do we do about it?
PRINCESS	Read the P.S.
KING	Eh? Oh, the bit at the bottom. (Reading.) 'P.S. I'll settle for half-a-dozen new-laid gold eggs. Well, of all the cheek. I remember that too. That's all he ever does ask for. Ridiculous, a measly half-dozen instead of you. My only kith and kin. Well, my only kith and kin now. You see -
PRINCESS	Ah, I know what you're going to say.
KING	You do?
PRINCESS	Yes. (To Audience.) It's an IMPORTANT BIT. But supposing you forget something, Daddy?
KING	Ah, it's so important I've make some notes. (To M.D.) Can I have them, please?

MUSIC 8   THE WHOLE STORY IN AN EGGSHELL

KING	When I was a little boy and very free from sin, I had a little brother, and my brother was my twin. He wasn't very handsome, not the slightest bit like me, And he became the bad egg of the royal family.
KING & PRINCESS	Now I am/you are quite a darling, as I think we all agree, But he became the bad egg of the royal family.
KING	There wasn't room for both of us to sit upon the throne, And my naughty little brother tried to sit on it alone. I didn't like to do it, but one nasty rainy day I sent him into exile half a million miles away.
KING & PRINCESS	You/I understand my/your sorrow when I/you pipe my/your eye and say I/You sent him into exile half a million miles away.
KING	Although he was a villain I liked Egbert just the same, And when I had my baby son I gave him Egbert's

	name. I hoped to have my baby's name upon the Honours Roll, But twenty years ago my little Egbert he was stole.
KING & PRINCESS	You/I understand I/you really was/were in something of a hole, When twenty years ago our little Egbert he was stole.
KING	I never will forget the time when he was stole away, For this Egg appeared upon this wall that very self- same day. If ever I forget to wear this noted look of pain, I just look at this Egg and I remember him again.

KING &
PRINCESS
	We looked for him and looked for him and looked for
	            him in vain –
	Now we just look at this Egg and we remember him
	            again.

KING	Of course there is a moral, now my sorry tale is
	            done:
	If you've an exiled brother and a stolen baby son,
	If you're a king and things like this should ever you
	            befall,
	Just look and see if there's an egg that's sitting on a
	            wall.

KING &
PRINCESS
	For psychiatric treatment, be your troubles great or
	            small,
	Just look and see if there's an egg that's sitting on a
	            wall.

	(Loud neighing off L.)
KING	Ah, here's our horses.
	(RANK and FILE enter L. on all fours with saddles strapped on their backs.)
RANK	(talking back as he enters) See, like this, nothing to it.
KING	They've shrunk.
RANK	Oh, your Majesty! (Straightens into kneeling position and salutes smartly.) Sir! File, kneel to attention.
	(FILE does.)

HUMPTY DUMPTY 13

                The 'orses is a little saddle shy, sir, so we're just demonstrating 'ow easy it is.

                (Neighing off L. again.)

                'Ere they are now.

                MUSIC 9

                (DOT, a skittish mare prances on. She has long eyelashes and wears a flowered straw hat.)

PRINCESS   Good morning, Dot.

                (CARRYONE lumbers on. He wears a soldier's hat.)

                And Carryone.

                (DOT does an elegant curtsey and CARRYONE crosses one foreleg over the other and nods.)

RANK   Right, come over 'ere, both of you, and hobserve closely.

                (RANK and FILE take up positions on all fours facing out front. DOT and CARRYONE come in between them.)

                Now, we 'ave got these nice comfy saddles on our backs, so we are you, right?

                (HORSES nod.)

                Right. Next watch 'ow 'is Majesty and 'er 'Ighness gently lower their royal –

                (KING and PRINCESS start to sit.)

                selves onto same. Right?

                (KING sits astride RANK and PRINCESS sidesaddle on FILE. HORSES nod.)

                Right.

                (KING and PRINCESS rise.)

                So now you know what to do. Right?

                (HORSES nod.)

                Right.

                (DOT sits on RANK and CARRYONE on FILE, who both collapse.)

FILE	Wrong!
RANK	You 'orrible little 'orses! Gerr off!
	(DOT and CARRYONE prance away to either side, DOT neighing with laughter. RANK and FILE rise and join the KING and PRINCESS in a huddled group C.)
KING	I don't think they quite understood. But what can we do now?
PRINCESS	(whispering) I think we should - well, sort of surprise them.
	(HORSES strain to hear and creep in to the group.)
KING	(whispering) Surprise them? How?
FILE	(whispering) I know, you could jump up and ride them without anything on at all.
KING	We don't want to surprise 'em that much!
PRINCESS	(whispering) Ssh! He means, ride them bareback, Daddy. Let's try.
	(RANK cups his hands for the PRINCESS to mount DOT and FILE cups his hands for the KING to mount CARRYONE. Their attempts are foiled by the back legs of each horse closing up to the front legs and standing upright.)
KING	I didn't know we had a camel corps.
	(DOT laughs. RANK and FILE pull them out again so that the horses are in profile with DOT facing R. and CARRYONE L.)
RANK	Ho, very funny.
PRINCESS	(whispering to KING) Let's leapfrog on from behind. They won't expect that.
	(They move to do so. The backlegs step in to the front legs and do a knees bend at the same time. The KING, who has made the more energetic leap, lands on the floor. DOT laughs. PRINCESS helps KING up. RANK and FILE sort the HORSES into shape again so that they are standing facing straight out.)

HUMPTY DUMPTY

RANK
: Ho, 'ighly 'umorous.

PRINCESS
: Let's try from the side again.

(She attempts to mount on DOT's L. side and the KING on CARRYONE's R., but the backlegs move away from them until the HORSES are completely 'U' shaped, i.e., both their frontsides and backsides are facing out front.)

I wonder whether they're coming or going?

(HORSES neigh, unravel themselves and run crossing each other for DOT to exit L. and CARRYONE R.)

FILE
: They're going.

RANK
: Quick! After 'em!

PRINCESS
: Leave Dot to me!   (Runs off L.)

FILE
: How kind, thank you so –

RANK
: Never mind that, come on!

(He shoves FILE to R.)

FILE
: Oh, Sergeant, you are so rough sometimes.

(They run off R.)

KING
: Pity, now I've got nothing to do; but there must be something – good gracious! Yes! Eiderdown! I mean, Underdown. I must get some gold eggs to send him. Where's what's-her-name – the chief chicken maid – er – what's she called, oh, er –

(Wanders off L. CARRYONE runs on R. with RANK grasping his tail, which he pulls on so that they stop C. and run on the spot.)

RANK
: Come along, you lot should have been able to help 'is Majesty. I told you to note the chief chicken-maid's name. It's 'Etty 'Encake. What is it? (Reaction.)   Well, don't keep it a secret. I said, what is it?   (Reaction.)   That's better. Once more for luck. What is it?

(As the reaction comes he is whipped off L. by CARRYONE.)

HETTY
: (off right.)   Coming! Coming!

HUMPTY DUMPTY — Sc. 1

MUSIC 10

(HETTY belts on from R. and slides to a stop. She carries a very small shopping basket.)

I'm here! But where are you? Oh, all down there in the chicken run. Lots of lovely little chicks, I see. A few old broilers, as well. Oh, and there's a very handsome rooster! How do you doodle-doodle-do, sir? You did catch my name I hope - Hetty Hencake.

(CARRYONE and RANK return from L. and again RANK pulls his tail and they run on the spot.)

RANK   Ah, Miss 'Encake. I'm afraid I got to report your chicken-girls for kissing and canoodling with my soldiers while on hescort duty.

HETTY   Really? How love - I mean, how dreadful. Kissing and canoodling? Hm. (Touching up her hair ruminatively.) I think I'll take over the escort duty myself.

RANK   Oh yes, miss. That'll stop any kissing and canoodling.

(CARRYONE yanks him off R.)

HETTY   Well, really! Oh, the weight of this is killing me. (Puts basket down with her behind pointing to R.)

(FILE runs on D.R.)

FILE   (grabbing HETTY's behind) Ah, got you!

HETTY   At last!

FILE   Oh, beg pardon. I thought you were a horse. (Runs off L.)

HETTY   I've gone right off soldiers. Anyway, I'm in a bit of a tizz-wozz today. I've discovered the most dreadful thing. You see, I'd just finished hoovering out the hen-coop, and what do you think I found? Nothing! That's what's so dreadful. I really must tell the King at once.

(KING enters L.)

Well, what a coincidence. (Curtseys.) Your

HUMPTY DUMPTY

	Majesticals. I'm afraid I've got some bad news. The hens have stopped laying gold eggs.
KING	What? But this is dreadful. They must have been bewitched. What can we do? Who can we turn to? (He is right beside ALBUMENIA's house.) Of course! Albamenia, the White Witch! She warned me about the egg. She'll help.
	(Pulls bellpull. <u>Effect 1. Huge sound of a church bell</u>. The reverberations shudder through the KING and HETTY. They look expectantly at the door.)
	Perhaps she's out.
HETTY	She'd hear that even if she was.
	(Wooden arm comes out from side of house with notice: 'I AM OUT'.)
	See? She did.
KING	But I must have half a dozen gold eggs for Underwear.
HETTY	Sounds uncomfortable.
KING	I mean, Underdown. You're the Keeper of the Privy Nest Egg, so what's the state of the Eggschequer?
HETTY	Well, I'll have a look. The Privy Nest Egg's in here somewhere. (Places basket on tub table.) There's one or two other things in here too. (Takes from basket large folded shopping bag.) You hold my spare bag and I'll pop 'em in.
	(The basket has no base and has in fact only contained the bag. The following articles are fed up through a trap in the tub table. HETTY takes them 'out' of the basket and chucks them into the bag which the KING holds open.)
	Now there's some tea, coffee, cocoa, sugar. And here's some liquorice allsorts, some jelly babies, some wine gums, oh, and these are new, very tasty - Guinness gums. Now the veg. Bunch of carrots, bunch of radishes, (Second bunch.) radishes, (Third bunch.) radishes.

KING	You're repeating yourself.
HETTY	Of course, they're radishes. Now the bread. (Long French loaf.) A yard of tripe. Two of sausages (Very long string of them.) spaghetti, pair of needles to knit it with (Large wooden ones.) and (A double toilet-roll.) - That reminds me, I must write to Mother. Well, that's all.
KING	(looks in puzzled disbelief between the basket and his now very full bag) All?
HETTY	Yes, you can't expect a little basket like this to hold much. Ah, wait a minute, I've forgotten the Privy Nest Egg. (Takes out nest with 12 gold eggs in it.) Ooh, there's only a dozen eggs left.
KING	Oh dear, and I've got to have half a dozen. (Takes them.) So that leaves - er - well, I can't waste time on a tricky problem like that. I'll get these off to Underdown and then have a good worry about the future - if only I can remember long enough to know what I'm worrying about. (Exit L. taking shopping bag.)
HETTY	Well, I'm a bit worried now. However can I guard this safely? (Suddenly hits forehead hard and staggers back.) Aaaah! It's all right, I'm not ill, I'm just staggered by my own brilliance. <u>I'm going to get you to look after it!</u> Ah, that surprised you, eh? But where can I put it? Well, I never - a shelf. (Puts nest egg on shelf in front of L. pros. arch.) Might have been put there on purpose. Now, if anyone tries to steal it I want all the little girls to cluck like hens and all the little boys to crow like roosters. We'll try it separately first. Right girls, let's hear you cluck. (Reaction.) Oh, I say, you have known some funny hens, I'm sure I heard a quack. I tell you what then, girls, you shout, 'Cluck-cluck-cluck!' Ready - go! (Reaction.) Oh, much better. In fact, I think somebody actually laid an egg. Now the boys. What does a rooster say when he crows? (Reaction.) Yes, some of you have got the idea - cock-a-doodle-do. But wait a minute, if you say cock-a-doodle-do people might think it's all right to take the nest egg. So you'd

better say, 'Cock-a-doodle-don't'. Let's hear that, ready - go! (Reaction.) Lovely! Let's put the two together. I'll pretend to steal the nest egg and all the little girls and boys must cluck and crow as loud as they can - all the little girls and boys under ninety, that is. (Moves to nest egg. Reaction.) Ah, that little boy over there, not a sound. You're not over ninety, are you? Are you? Well, you don't look a day over eighty-nine. And I'm sure that little girl there is hardly eighty-eight yet. What's that, dear? You're worried about your tea? Oh, your teeth. Well, take 'em out. Hens don't have teeth, anyway. Just one last practice then. (Moves to nest egg. Reaction.) Marvellous! But then, I've always had a way with children. In fact, in fact, IN FACT - I keep saying in fact like that 'cos this is my IMPORTANT BIT, so I hope you've all got your pencils ready. In fact, I started in the royal service as Nursemaid to Little Egbert. That's it. (To M.D.) No, only one 'g' in Egbert, dear. Two 't's' in little. But now you can forget about it for the next couple of hours and then - oh, you will be surprised. (To Audience.) Anyway, I've always found with children you must give them a chance to let themselves go. It's very good for grown-ups, too. You see -

MUSIC 11 TOP OF THE WORLD

In ancient Greece a learned man
   Of misery would speak;
But you'd be miserable too
   If you had to write in Greek;
But he found a solution
   For the bother and the fuss.
The moral that he left us
   Is translated roughly thus:-

Bang, bash, clatter and crash!
   Throw yourself about.
If you whisper
   They won't hear you shout.
Bang, bash, clatter and crash!
   Keep the flag unfurled.

Bang, bash, clatter and crash!
You'll be on top of the world.

Nowadays I never let
　The miseries occur,
'Cos that's the thought I've always thunk
　When I am feeling 'Ugh!'
So if the weather's horrible
　And life is running slow,
The best advice that I can give
　Is sing fortissimo -
Bang, bash, etc.

(HETTY exits, with her little shopping basket, into the Inn.)

MUSIC 12

(There is a commotion off R. and ROMANO, a romantic looking Gipsy, enters with the CHICKEN-MAIDS holding his arms and the SOLDIERS remonstrating with him.)

SOLDIERS and CHICKEN-MAIDS Be off! No gipsies in Goldova. They're not allowed! We shall arrest you. It's the King's orders, etc.

Don't be so silly! What's it matter? Don't be so bossy! You're just jealous! We like him, etc.

ROMANO　Thank you, ladies. But why all the fuss, gentlemen?

2nd SOLDIER　It's by order of the King.

1st SOLDIER　Gipsies aren't allowed in the Kingdom.

ROMANO　Ah, but the World is our kingdom, and there we have as much right as you. And why not? We're not really all that different, you know.

MUSIC 13 SO CAN I

If you have two eyes that see,
　Then so have I.
If you've feet to wander free,
　Then so have I.
If you feel you can demand
Your portion of the promised land
　And freely walk beneath a boundless sky,
　Then so can I.

Not the city's sorrows and its strife for me,
Seeking all that's gentle is the life for me.
If you are of humble birth
And still can be the lords of the earth,
Then so can I, so can I, so can I.

Though you try to cheat me,
  Laugh at me and spurn me,
Here's a spirit you can never kill.
From the road I've chosen
  You will never turn me,
I will take whatever path I will,
And that will be
  My destiny.

If you have two eyes, etc.

1st SOLDIER Well, maybe it'll be all right.

2nd SOLDIER If you don't say around too long.

ROMANO Thank you, and while we're here why not come to our gipsy camp? We'll sing for you, dance for you, tell the fortunes of these pretty ladies -

(Pleased reaction from GIRLS.)

and show you our horses, our fine gipsy horses, so swift, so sleek, so surefooted, like -

(DOT bolts on D.L., neighing loudly.)

Well, not like that.

PRINCESS (off L.) Stop her somebody! Hold her!

(The SOLDIERS try to do so but DOT rampages around, charging at them and kicks out front and rear legs till she puts all, except ROMANO, to flight. Very pleased with herself, she gives her neighing laugh just as the PRINCESS runs on L.)

You naughty girl! Come here at once.

(DOT tosses her head and starts to run R.)

ROMANO Ah-ah! Do as the lady says.

(DOT stops in surprise then starts to paw the ground ferociously as he advances towards her.)

Gently, girl, gently.

(Her pawing tails away. He strokes her head, she flutters her eyelids and rubs her head against him.)

That's better. Now off you go back to your stable.

(He gives her a friendly pat on her rump. She wiggles her rear and gives a little whinny of delight, waves a farewell hoof and trots off L.)

PRINCESS Well, you certainly have a way with horses.

ROMANO Ah well, I'm a gipsy.

PRINCESS Are you? I've never seen one before. You see, my father doesn't like gipsies.

ROMANO He's not the only one round here then. I understand the King doesn't like them either.

PRINCESS Well, he is the King actually. It's because of little Egbert.

ROMANO Little Egbert?

PRINCESS Yes, he was Daddy's son but he disappeared when he was a baby and just because some gipsies happened to be camped nearby at the time, he - well - he -

ROMANO He thought the gipsies stole him? Yes, we're always being blamed for stealing babies.

PRINCESS But I'm quite sure you wouldn't steal any babies Mr - er?

ROMANO Romano but not Mr - just Romano.

PRINCESS Romano? I rather like that. (Sighs.) What a pity you won't be allowed to stay here, because - (Catches his eye and looks away.)

ROMANO Because?

PRINCESS Oh, nothing.

ROMANO I think I know the sort of nothing you mean.

MUSIC 14 SWEET NOTHING

There is nothing I can make a song about;
When you fall in love the words just won't come out.

	What occurs to all the thoughts you would recall? Sweet nothing at all.
PRINCESS	Ev'ry word of love that I should try to sing Turns into an incoherent babberling. All the biggest things in life become so small - Sweet nothing at all.
ROMANO	Well, that is - I mean to say -
PRINCESS	What an awful lot of scandal there has been -
ROMANO	What good books - ?
PRINCESS	A lovely day -
BOTH	Surely you must know exactly what I mean!
ROMANO	I would like to sit and write some poetry;
PRINCESS	Just a sonnet would be quite enough for me;
BOTH	But the moment when my Muse should pay a call - Sweet nothing at all. Sweet nothing at all. Sweet nothing at all.

(They exit.)

<u>MUSIC 15</u>

(ALBUMENIA, the White Witch, enters R. astride a broomstick from which 'L' plates dangle down. She is dressed as a witch with steeple hat, etc, but all in white.)

ALBUMENIA	Oh, how provoking! What a bore, I've fail'd my flying test once more. I'm Albumenia, my dears, A witch, but white, so have no fears, For with black magic I've no truck - Except these chocs!

(Produces a large box of 'Black Magic' chocolates and takes one.)

Um, scrumptious tuck!
But now to matters less delicious.
(Addresses House.) Anyone call'd?

(Arm comes from side of house with sign - 'YES'.)

Re what?

(A stream of ticker-tape shoots out of letter-box. She tears off a strip and reads.)

    How vicious!
Someone's nobbled the gilt-edged chicks!
Now who would play such filthy tricks?
Why, wicked Wizard Fowlpest would.
He'd win this kingdom if he could;
'Twas he, who years ago, I fear,
Made little Egbert disappear,
Because next day I thought it shady
That Fowlpest should become a lady -
Well, more a crone, call'd Ancient Alice
Who for years sold eggs at the Palace.
Thus disguis'd he sneak'd through the gate
But deep within his eggy freight
He'd hidden - No, best not to tell;
Suffice to say, I cast a spell
Which hid what he'd hid, only more,
Inside an egg. And I'm quite sure
That there it's stay'd for twenty years,
(Points to Egg on wall.)
'Cos that's the egg it's in, my dears!
And though I know I shouldn't crow
I could wish for a worthier foe.
Fowlpest's so crude and what is worse
He speaks such rotten rhyming verse,
Which is, of course, the thing that tells
In casting really first-class spells.
Even so, the hens have stopp'd laying,
So I must find what game he's playing.
And as time's flying so will I,
Or rather, I shall have a try.
Oh, here take these.

(House door swings open. She hands in the 'Black Magic' chocolates but immediately a large box of Cadbury's 'Milk Tray' is handed out.)

    What's this? Milk Tray?
No, no, for flying, chocs away!

(Hands back box and door shuts.)

The hens I hope I'll soon put right

HUMPTY DUMPTY

'Cos sometimes Fowlpest's none too bright.
Why even now he doesn't know
Just where I made his secret go.
(As she moves away broomstick rears up.)
Oops, steady dear.   (Exit R.)

(Flash L.)

MUSIC 16

(FOWLPEST, a rather seedy-looking wizard, enters L. from behind Inn.)

FOWLPEST   Aha! You're wrong, my would-be bird,
For every word I overheard.
Yes I, Fowlpest, whom she'll soon see
Makes all too good an enemy.
In fact a Witch of her poor fibre
Don't merit one of my calibre.   (Correct pronun-
                                              ciation.)
Hrmm – or even one of by ca_li_bre.
And yet she mocks my rhyming verse,
Which plainly is ri_di_cu - lerse.
The only thing is that my scansion
I don't like to make too rigid so that it allows plenty
              of room for expansion.
But that is just poetic licence,
A handy phrase that's – er – that's –

that's rather silly because you can't get anything to rhyme with it. Anyway, rhyming verse is only necessary for casting really tricky spells; it's just showing off to use it all the time. That's typical of Albumenia, though. I'm rather more modest myself, even though I'm so clever. Well, you'll see for now at last my triumph's nigh! At last I can –

(CHICKWEED, a witchlet, who wears a little steeple hat perched saucily on top of her head and a short cloak on her shoulders runs on excitedly from L.)

CHICKWEED   Wheeeee!

(She grabs his hand and whirls him round.)

FOWLPEST   Chickweed!

CHICKWEED	I did it, Mr Fowlpest, I did it! I did it! I did it! Wheeeee!
FOWLPEST	Stop! I'm getting dizzy, leggo! (Disengages himself.) Really, Chickweed, that's no way for an apprentice witchlet to treat her master.
CHICKWEED	(hugging him impetuously) Splendid master! Clever master! You taught me and I did it! (Jumping up and down with him.) I did it! I did it! I did it!
FOWLPEST	(overlapping) Stop it! Put me down! I'll - I'll cast a spell on you!
CHICKWEED	(releases him) But that's what I did! I cast a spell! My first solo spell! And it worked! I hexed the hens! I bewitched 'em! I put my evil eye on them! Well, it's not really evil yet, but it's quite naughty! And it worked! They can't lay any more gold eggs! (Throwing hat off L.) Whoopee!
FOWLPEST	QUIET! Foolish girl. (Indicates ALBUMENIA's house apprehensively.) Walls have ears, you know.
	(U.S. window shutter swings open and reveals a large ear on its reverse side. (Shutter operated by a nylon line running offstage.))
CHICKWEED	Ooh! So do window-shutters.
FOWLPEST	Eh? Well, there, now look what you've done.
CHICKWEED	Sorry, Mr Fowlpest. Shall I go and - ?
FOWLPEST	(martyred) No, no. Leave it to me. (Whispering conspiratorially.) I shall conjure up an ear plug.
CHICKWEED	Oh, Mr Fowlpest, you are so clever.
FOWLPEST	Yes. Yes, I am. But this will be quite simple, just a magic pass or two - (Makes passes with his hands.) and hey presto! we have - (Produces a trick bouquet, which surprises him but he recovers quickly.) Hm. We have a little something to congratulate you on your first spell. (Presents it.)

HUMPTY DUMPTY

CHICKWEED Oh, Mr Fowlpest, you shouldn't have.

FOWLPEST No, I shouldn't. I mean - Anyway, the ear plug.

(CHICKWEED creeps over to house.)

Let's see. (Puts up a hand to take off his pointed hat.) No, I might have brought some rabbits with me. Er - ear plug - (Notices CHICKWEED.) What are you doing?

CHICKWEED (turns to put a finger to her lips, then turns back and leans very close to ear) BOO!

(Shutter snaps shut and CHICKWEED quickly puts latch on.)

There!

FOWLPEST Hm. Yes. Well, of course, that's what I hoped you'd do. I was testing you. Hm. But now to more important matters. Listen. Once I had - well, something very precious to me and Albumenia hid it. But now, after a mere twenty years searching, I have found out where - in that Egg up there!

CHICKWEED Golly!

FOWLPEST Golly indeed, for it's through what's in that Egg that I shall win the Kingdom to my rule at last!

CHICKWEED How super!

FOWLPEST Yes, but first I must break open the Egg, so I shall cast a very special spell to knock it off the wall. You'd better put your hat on for it.

(CHICKWEED exits momentarily L. to do so. The hat has had an invisible line attached to it and a similar line is fixed to the collar of her cloak.)

Can't have you improperly dressed. I'm going to use rhyming verse.

CHICKWEED (returning) Oh dear, I know you're awfully clever, Mr Fowlpest, but are you sure rhyming verse is a good idea?

FOWLPEST Quite certain. I've got a new system.

For rhymes that are especially tricky
I now have got a rhyming dicky.

CHICKWEED	A rhyming dicky? Ah, a rhyming dictionary.
FOWLPEST	No, a rhyming dicky. (Pulls off shirt front.) There. Let's see. (Consults it.) Got it! Right, stand by.

Abracadabra may be old hat
But off you'll come in spite of that.

(Makes a magic pass at Egg. <u>Swanee whistle</u> as CHICKWEED's hat flies off.)

Hm, odd. (Consults shirt front again.) Perhaps this'll be better.

I shroud a spell in myst'ry's cloak
And off you'll whisk when I have spoke!

(Makes pass again, <u>Swanee whistle</u> as CHICKWEED's cloak flies off.)

Very strange. (Consults shirt front again.) Ah, this is the ticket.

Magic surround you like a skirt –

(CHICKWEED looks apprehensive and grabs her skirt waist. HETTY steps out of Inn door as FOWLPEST speaks next line.)

And down you'll fall, I'll bet my shirt.

(Makes pass. <u>Swanee whistle</u>. HETTY's skirt falls down (pulled from behind). She gives a cry and rushes back into Inn with it. As she entered below FOWLPEST and CHICKWEED, apparently neither saw her.)

Funny, nothing happened at all. One last try.

CHICKWEED	But Mr Fowlpest, why can't we just push it – like this!

(She gives the Egg a push and it starts to rock.)

<u>MUSIC 17</u>

FOWLPEST	How dull.
RANK	(off R.) Army, quick march!
FOWLPEST	The army! Let's beat a hasty retreat.

HUMPTY DUMPTY

(They start to run off D.L.)

CHICKWEED   Ooh, look! Gold eggs.

FOWLPEST   Always useful. We'll take them.

(Audience reaction.)

We won't.

(They exit D.L.)

HETTY   (off in Inn) Coming! Coming! (Runs on, beskirted again.) Sorry, I had such a tussle with my bustle and – my goodness! The Egg! (Rushing to and fro.) Help! Help!

(CHICKEN-MAIDS run on L.)

CHICK MAIDS   The Egg!

(KING enters L.)

KING   What's all this hullabaloo?

HETTY & CHICK MAIDS   Look!

KING   The Egg! It's falling! Send for my horses! Send for my men!

HETTY   The King's horses!

(DOT and CARRYONE run on L.)

CHICK MAIDS   The King's men!

(RANK and FILE and SOLDIERS run on R.)

KING   Save it! Save the Egg to save my crown!

(The MILITARY run to and fro with the motion of the Egg.)

MILITARY   We can't!

ALL   It's going – going!

(BLACKOUT and loud drum crash.)

Gone!

(LIGHTS UP. Egg has gone from wall and HUMPTY DUMPTY, a comical looking little fellow is sitting spread-eagled at the foot of it

HUMPTY DUMPTY — Sc. 1

with everyone staring at him, except the KING, who stands apart D. S. with the HORSES, holding firmly on to his crown.

ALL Ooh!

KING What is it?

RANK It's a person-shaped hobject, sir.

KING It's a what?

HETTY It's a man!

SOLDIERS A bloke!

CHICK MAIDS A feller!

FILE A chap!

KING (to HORSES)   Any comment?

HORSES (shaking heads)   Ne-igh!

KING So, then it's –   (Turns.)

HUMPTY It's just me.

KING A likely story! I know me and I'm him. You impostor! What's your real name?

HUMPTY Ah, there you have me. I'm not sure. Falling off that wall's made me feel all humpty-dumpty.

HETTY Yes, dear, you look a bit humpty-dumpty, too.

HUMPTY Do I? Well, perhaps I should be Humpty Dumpty then. I'll just try it for size. Humpty Dumpty. Yes – yes, I like it. Humpty Dumpty. Oh yes, it's me to a T. I can feel it all over me. All Humpty and Dumpty. I'll take it. Don't bother to wrap it, I'll keep it on.

KING Have you quite finished?

HUMPTY Sorry. I got rather used to talking to myself, living in an egg. You don't meet many people in an egg. In fact, you don't meet any. So it's jolly nice to be out of it and to meet some now.
(To others.)   Hullo, people.

OTHERS Hullo, Humpty Dumpty.

HUMPTY	Ooh, I like that. Have you got any other people anywhere?
HETTY	Yes, dear, there's one or two over here.
	(Leads him D.C.)
	(HOUSE LIGHTS UP.)
HUMPTY	Gosh! There's - (Pretends to count rapidly.) exactly five hundred people. (Or whatever is appropriate.) Hullo, exactly five hundred people.
	(Reaction. HETTY encourages Audience to reply.)
	Marvellous! Oh, I am glad to be out of that egg.
	(HOUSE OUT.)
KING	That's a pity because I'm afraid you'll have to go back in it. Sergeant Rank, see that he's put together again.
RANK	Ye - put together, sir?
KING	Yes, surely all the King's horses and all the King's men can manage a simple little thing like that.
	(DOT gives her neighing laugh and runs off L. with CARRYONE.)
	What a coarse horse. Anyway, if you'd guarded the Egg properly it wouldn't have happened. And just how did it happen?
	(PRINCESS enters with ROMANO R.)
PRINCESS	Daddy, I know you don't like gipsies, but -
KING	Gipsies! That's it! There's the culprit, seize him!
RANK	(salutes) Sir! File, Atkins, arrest that gipsy!
	(FILE and 1st SOLDIER arrest ROMANO, despite loud protests from him and the PRINCESS.)
KING	Enough! Take him and throw him in our deepest dungeon!
RANK	Yes, sir! Prisoner and escort, to the deepest dungeon, quick march!

FILE	But we haven't got any dungeons, not even shallow ones.
RANK	Then we'll himprovise! Quick march!
	(He exits L. with ROMANO and his escort.)
PRINCESS	But, Daddy, Romano didn't touch the Egg. Oh – who's this?
HUMPTY	Hullo. I'm Humpty Dumpty. I was in the Egg.
KING	Yes, and he'll have to be put back in it somehow.
PRINCESS	What – in all that broken shell? (Laughs.) That's ridiculous, especially as he seems quite harmless.
HUMPTY	Oh, thank you. All the people I meet get nicer and nicer.
KING	He may seem harmless. But what about my crown, eh? (Takes it off and points to it.) You want it, don't you?
HUMPTY	No, it looks rather a draughty kind of hat to me. The only thing I want at the moment is food. Any food, so long as it's not eggs because that's all I had to eat in there – egg-yolk.
HETTY	Yes, that does sound a bit of a bind. What do you fancy then?
HUMPTY	As it's such a special day for me, I'd like a cake, a great big sort of birthday cake.
PRINCESS	Why, is it your birthday too?
HUMPTY	No, it's my un-birthday. They're much better. You only get one birthday a year but three hundred and sixty-four un-birthdays. There's glory for you!
HETTY	How true, and now you come to mention it, it's my un-birthday, too.
PRINCESS	It's mine as well!
CHORUS	And mine!
KING	Well, as I never can remember when my birthday is, it's probably mine too. All right, you can stay out while we all have a great big un-birthday party.

HUMPTY DUMPTY

ALL	Hooray!
	MUSIC 18 ANY EXCUSE FOR A PARTY
HUMPTY	Today isn't anyone's birthday,
KING	Nobody's passed an exam.
PRINCESS	No one we know's getting married,
HETTY	And nobody's buying a pram.
ALL	So let's have a great celebration,
	Let's have a wonderful ball,
	'Cos any excuse for a party
	Is better than nothing at all.
HUMPTY	Since one has to be careful
	Of all the things one eats,
	I am on a strict diet
	Of hamburgers, ice-cream, fishfingers and trifle,
	potato crisps, pork pies and jellies and baked beans and sweets!
ALL	Today isn't anyone's birthday,
	Nobody's passed an exam.
	No one we know's getting married,
	And nobody's buying a pram.
	So let's have a great celebration,
	Let's have a wonderful ball,
	'Cos any excuse for a party
	Is better than nothing at all.
	Somebody roll out the barrel;
	Let's wear our party apparel,
	'Cos any excuse for a party
	Is better, is better, is better than nothing at all.
	(ALL exit L. FADE LIGHTS except on ALBUMENIA's house. Smoke starts to puff out of the chimney. (See 'Special Instructions' at end of text.))
ALBUMENIA	(off R.) Coming! Coming!
	MUSIC 19
	(She runs on on her broomstick.) All right, I'm here, don't get too fussed. Now what's gone wrong?

(Arm comes out with sign – 'LOOK AT THE WALL'. She does.)

      The Egg's been bust!
So! Fowlpest's done his worst again.
Come, Albumenia, to his den!

(She runs on the spot. FADE LIGHTS and start STROBE FREEZE LIGHT. As she 'runs' drop in Scene 2 cloth behind her. (If a FREEZE LIGHT is not used ALBUMENIA should be held in the light of a single spot as she 'runs' and the cloth is dropped in.))

Scene Two: The Wizard's Den

Frontcloth.

When the cloth is in FADE FREEZE LIGHT, FADE UP SCENE LIGHTS.

ALBUMENIA stops running and pants heavily.

ALBUMENIA Whew! I'm there. Now unseen I'll lurk
And hear what further filthy work
The frightful Fowlpest has in mind.
(Looks round.)
Nowhere to lurk, though. What a bind.
But wait! Yes! Yes! Surprise, surprise!
I'll disappear before your eyes.
(Starts making magic passes.)
Self, begone!
(Hits head with broomstick handle rather too hard.)

MUSIC 20

(Sting and flash.)

     Ow! My sainted aunt!
But as you see, or rather can't,

	That since I gave myself that wham, I'm quite invisible. I am! Oh, yes I am! (Reaction.) Oh, yes I am! (Reaction.) Well, what a disbelieving lot But as you seem so unimpress'd To prove it I shall steal the nest. (Moves towards it. Reaction. HETTY runs on R.)
HETTY	Aha! Caught you, you naughty – oh, naughty nobody. (Moves to go and is stopped by Audience.) What's that? There is somebody? (Looks all round stage.) There isn't. You're having me on. Well, Where are they then? (ALBUMENIA stands close beside her on her L.) Right beside me? (Turns to R.) Well, there's nobody this side. The other side? (Turns to L. and looks through ALBUMENIA.) There's even more nobody this side. Ah, I know how to settle it. I'll ask the boys down here. I can always trust them. (To Orchestra.) Is there anybody here, boys?
ORCHESTRA	Yes!
HETTY	Well, that proves it. (Starts to go, stops at R. exit.) What's the matter now? I said I can always trust them and I can. I can always trust them to tell fibs. (Exit R.)
ALBUMENIA	There now, she couldn't see a trace I'm visually a vacant space. (Cups a hand to L. ear.) And just as well, from not far distant Come Fowlpest and his young assistant. (FOWLPEST and CHICKWEED run on L., and to ALBUMENIA's surprise, though they do not realise her presence, dance excitedly round her.)
FOWLPEST & CHICKWEED	Wheeeee! We did it! We did it, we did it, we did it! (They stop on either side of her.)
FOWLPEST	Silly old Albumenia! There was the Egg –

36 HUMPTY DUMPTY Sc. 2

CHICKWEED: On the wall –

FOWLPEST: Right outside her house –

CHICKWEED: But so were we –

BOTH: (leaning forward to suit the action to the word) Right under her nose!

FOWLPEST: And where's the Egg now?

BOTH: Broken in bits!

(They join hands encircling ALBUMENIA and jump up and down so that she is forced to jump with them.)

Broken in bits, broken in bits, in lots and lots of tiny bits!

FOWLPEST: And at last Humpty Dumpty is free! Of course, that's not his real name, but no matter.

CHICKWEED: What is his real name? It's not little Egbert is it?

FOWLPEST: Certainly not. Little Egbert – (Confidentially.) I'm the one who got rid of Little Egbert.

CHICKWEED: Oh, Mr Fowlpest, did you actually –

FOWLPEST: No, no, I mean I got rid of him out of the kingdom, that's all. That's why years ago I tried to smuggle Humpty into the Palace. I meant to put him in Little Egbert's place so that he would have grown up to be King and I could have controlled the Kingdom through him. But now I shall put my new plan into action. I'm going to give him something. (Puts a hand off L. and brings on a fishing rod. It has no line.)

CHICKWEED: A fish?

FOWLPEST: No, no. I'm going to give him a magic wish – so that he can wish himself to be King. This is just my magic rod to bring him here.

CHICKWEED: But I can't see any line, Mr Fowlpest.

FOWLPEST: Of course not. It's a magic line with a magic hook. I cast it like this and –

(He 'casts' towards R. <u>Swanee whistle and bonk.</u> It evidently catches ALBUMENIA in rear. She gives a cry then slaps a hand to her mouth. FOWLPEST

HUMPTY DUMPTY

and CHICKWEED are puzzled by her cry.)

FOWLPEST: Strange noise. I think I've caught something, though.

(ALBUMENIA nods and mimes uncatching herself.)

But I can't see it.

(ALBUMENIA 'releases' herself. FOWLPEST who has been 'tugging', mimes the line coming free.)

Tcha! Lost it. I'll cast harder this time.

(He makes a powerful back-swing. <u>Swanee whistle</u> and <u>drum bonk</u> followed by a cry off L. as he tries to bring the rod forward.)

Now, what have I got caught on?

('Tugs' and 'drags' on HUMPTY backwards apparently by the seat of his pants.)

CHICKWEED: Mr Fowlpest you've got him! And oh - he's lovely!

HUMPTY: Who, me?

FOWLPEST: What are you burbling about? (Turns.) Oh. Yes, well I wasn't <u>quite</u> certain that back cast would work, but I haven't lost the knack, I see. Hum. Humpty Dumpty, I believe.

HUMPTY: Yes, but I'm sorry I can't turn round to say hallo. I seem to be caught up on something.

FOWLPEST: What? Oh, of course. Chickweed, release him.

CHICKWEED: Release him? Oh, please, can't we keep him?

FOWLPEST: Foolish girl. Release him from this. (Indicates rod.)

CHICKWEED: Oh! At once. (Doing so.) Poor Humpty Dumpty.

FOWLPEST: Now, put this away and bring me my wand.

CHICKWEED: All right. (To HUMPTY.) Be back in a flash. (She skips off L. with rod.)

FOWLPEST: She's behaving very oddly. Never mind - You're Humpty Dumpty, eh? Well, I'm -

(<u>Flash</u> and CHICKWEED skips on again with magic wand.)

	What are you doing?
CHICKWEED	I said I'd be back in a flash.
FOWLPEST	(taking wand pettishly) Tcha! Wasting good magic. Now Humpty, I'm your f -
	(ALBUMENIA listens intently.)
	(Aside.) No, I'll reveal that later. (To HUMPTY.) I'm your friendly neighbourhood wizard and -
CHICKWEED	And I'm Chickweed his even friendlier witchlet apprentice and I do hope you're pleased to meet me.
HUMPTY	Yes, you seem awfully, well, awfully -
CHICKWEED	Oh, I'm so glad I seem awfully.
FOWLPEST	Chickweed! Have you gone potty?
CHICKWEED	(gazing at HUMPTY) Completely!
FOWLPEST	Then go potty quietly. I have something to give Humpty.
HUMPTY	Really? Oh good. I'm rather hungry. I got dragged away from my un-birthday party somehow before I could get any un-birthday cake.
FOWLPEST	Oh, this is much better than cake. It's a Magic Wish! You'll be able to wish for anything in the world. Yes, even the King's crown! (Nudges him and winks heavily.) Here it comes. (Waving wand about.) Here create a magic wish Like a glittering silver - er - tish - splish? No. Silver? (Clicks fingers at CHICKWEED.)
CHICKWEED	(looking adoringly at HUMPTY) Dish.
FOWLPEST	No - like a glittering silver - er -
ALBUMENIA	(standing on far side of HUMPTY, unable to restrain herself) Fish!
FOWLPEST	(to HUMPTY) That's very good. I didn't see your lips move at all. And you're quite right. (Waves wand again and speaks rapidly.) Here create a magic wish,

Like a glittering silver fish.

MUSIC 21

(FOWLPEST produces a glittering silver ball. ALBUMENIA creeps round.)

Success! Look!

(ALBUMENIA grabs it and moves away.)

Aah! It's gone! Chickweed, stop gawking and help me find it.

(They and HUMPTY search around.)

ALBUMENIA (aside) Another's spell I can't revoke
But I can have my little joke.
(Makes a pass with one hand at 'wish'.)

MUSIC 22

(Sting.)

Now with this wish I wish you well –
If where to wish it you can tell!
(Throws down a glittering blue ball which she surreptitiously switched for the other and exits R.)

MUSIC 23

(HUMPTY catches the ball.)

HUMPTY Here it is! It looks a bit off colour, though.

FOWLPEST Off colour? (Takes 'wish'.) Do you know what this means?

HUMPTY Somebody's not using Persil?

FOWLPEST I don't wish to know that. It means somebody's got at it and I bet I know who. She's made it so it can only be wished at the end of the rainbow.

HUMPTY Pity. That's rather a tricky place to find.

FOWLPEST No, no, a mere temporary setback. We'll set out in search of it immediately. See you when we get back. Ta-ta for now.

HUMPTY Eh?

FOWLPEST Goodbye.

HUMPTY	Oh, good –
FOWLPEST	Exactly.

(Pushes him off R. and turns to CHICKWEED who is waving sadly.)

Chickweed, stop behaving like a broken railway signal and go and pack my magic rain gauge, my magic sun detector <u>and</u> my magic corn plasters.

CHICKWEED	Your magic corn plasters?
FOWLPEST	Yes, we're going to do a lot of walking. Magic is not always an easy path to tread. In fact sometimes it's decidedly tricky.

MUSIC 24 BONK!

Things can occur not far short of tragic
  If you are lacking in expertise.

CHICKWEED	If you start mucking about with magic, BONK! You're down on your knees.
FOWLPEST	Spells have a habit of boomeranging If you don't get them quite right at once.
CHICKWEED	Just throw them wrong and you'll feel the banging BONK! It's back on your bonce.

BOTH	You may argue that a
	Little error doesn't matter,
	  Or the kettle isn't always on the boil;
	But you'll soon become much wiser
	If each time you drink some Tizer
	  It turns out to be a dose of Castor Oil.

FOWLPEST	You should rehearse ev'ry incantation;
CHICKWEED	Always take care how you make a pass.
BOTH	One tiny lapse in your concentration – BONK! You've fallen down on the wayside.

(Dance.)

Once we knew a stinker,
A compulsive type of drinker
  Who would also eat immense amounts of grub.
Off the bottle we would lure him

	With a spell designed to cure him; But it didn't and he turned into a pub!
FOWLPEST	If you'd a client who has a notion He'd like to make an opponent droop,
CHICKWEED	One wrong ingredient in the potion -
BOTH	BONK! You're right in the - Fallen down in the - Right down splash in the soup!

(Close traverse tabs during number and fly cloth out.

BLACKOUT. Open traverse tabs.)

Scene Three: The Royal Cavalry Stables

Fullset. Cut-out across the back of three horse stalls labelled from R. to L. 'DOT', 'CARRYONE' and 'ACTING TEMPORARY DUNGEON' which has a huge padlock on it. Suitable wings L. and R. Each stall has a nosebag hanging beside it. The stall doors are hinged on the L. to open on-stage. There is a bridle lying on the floor.

FILE is discovered sweeping. DOT and CARRY-ONE are in their stalls.

FILE	(stopping and leaning on his broom) I feel just like Cinderella. Any moment now my Fairy Godmother will appear and say -
RANK	(marching on L.) File! Stop mucking about.
FILE	I'm not mucking about. I'm mucking out. Oh, look, Dot's dropped her hair net. (Picks up bridle.)
RANK	'Er 'air net? You noodle, don't you know a bridle when you see one?

FILE	Beg pardon?
RANK	I said - bridle!
FILE	Oh, very well. (Tosses his head vigorously.)
RANK	What are you doing now?
FILE	You just told me to bridle, so I am! (Tosses his head even more vigorously.)
RANK	No, no, no! This thing is <u>called</u> a bridle. You fix the reins to it. And this goes in the horse's mouth. It's called the bit.
FILE	The bit - is it important?
RANK	Very.
FILE	(to Audience) Ah, another important bit.
RANK	Not that kind of a bit! You'll get 'em all confused. Put it away. We must give the 'orses their breakfast.
FILE	Righto. (Hangs bridle on a convenient nail.) Come on, gee-gees, lovely brekkers. (HORSES put their heads eagerly over top of their stable doors. FILE gets a nosebag for CARRYONE.)
RANK	(taking a nosebag to hang over DOT's head) Not gee-gees - 'orses, and not brekkers - breakfast. Right, you two. Any complaints?
DOT	Neigh!
CARRYONE	Neigh! (HORSES retire into their stalls.)
RANK	Good. Now, give the prisoner 'is breakfast.
FILE	If you say so. (Shrugs and knocks on door of third stall.) Wakey! Wakey! Breakfast.
ROMANO	(putting his head over the top of his stall door) Breakfast? Good, I'm hungry.
FILE	Here you are then. (Puts third nosebag over his head.)
ROMANO	I'm not hungry.

RANK	(takes nosebag off) You nitwit! Not that sort of food. 'E's a prisoner, so 'e must be given proper prisoner's food - like bread and water.
FILE	Bread and water? But we haven't got any bread.
	(Enter PRINCESS R., carrying a cake on a plate.)
PRINCESS	Then let him eat cake.
	(RANK snaps to attention and salutes.)
	I've brought the prisoner an un-birthday cake. I'll feed it to him if you're busy.
RANK	That's very kind of Your 'Ighness, 'cos we are a bit pushed this morning. Your Royal Dad wants us to find some way to put 'Umpty Dumpty together again. (Salutes.) Come on, File. We'll see 'ow my glue's getting on.
FILE	All right but I'm sure my paste will be better.
	(They exit arguing L.)
PRINCESS	Hullo.
ROMANO	Hullo. It's funny, but now you're here I really don't feel hungry any more. Not for food anyway.
PRINCESS	Oh dear, that's a pity. Somebody's got to eat the cake or you'll never be able to escape.
	(HUMPTY enters R., sniffing appreciatively, with his eyes partially closed.)
HUMPTY	Cake, definitely cake, and a particularly yummy cake, too. (His nose 'homes' right onto the cake. Opens his eyes.) Ah! I was right. Oh, I shall enjoy this. (Is about to bite cake when he realises the PRINCESS is holding it.) Oh, sorry. I didn't realise it was your cake.
PRINCESS	Not at all, be my guest. You'll be helping me by eating it.
HUMPTY	Really? What a nice way to help someone. And I'd like to help you because you stopped your father putting me back in that egg. And also because - because -

PRINCESS	Because?
HUMPTY	Because you're - you're sort of - well, sort of you.
ROMANO	I know just what he means.
HUMPTY	Well, cheers! (Bites.) Ow! There's something in the cake. Something hard.
PRINCESS	Sorry, I should have warned you. But it seemed so suitable.
ROMANO	How do you mean?
PRINCESS	Well, you're a prisoner so of course I brought you a cake. And naturally inside it I'd hidden - (Pulling a tiny file from the piece of cake.) A file!
FILE	(looking on L.) Someone call?
PRINCESS	(hiding file) No, I said the weather's been vile.
FILE	Ah. (Goes.)
ROMANO	(taking file) I say, a file!
FILE	(looking on) Yes?
ROMANO	(hiding it) Er - yes the roof does need a tile.
FILE	Oh. (Goes.)
HUMPTY	(taking file) I see, a -
FILE	(looking on) Um?
HUMPTY	(hiding file) Wait a minute, I haven't said it yet.
FILE	Sorry. (Goes.)
HUMPTY	A file.
FILE	(looking on) Now?
	(HUMPTY nods and smiles at him.)
	Oh, what a nice smile. (Goes.)
HUMPTY	It's a very little -
	(ROMANO and PRINCESS put their fingers to their lips.)
	One of these things.

HUMPTY DUMPTY 45

PRINCESS	(taking it) But very efficient. (Files through padlock with one rasp. (Ratchet from drummer.)) See? He's free.
ROMANO	(opens stall door) Free!
PRINCESS	Where will you go?
ROMANO	To the Gipsy Camp. I'll be safe enough there.
PRINCESS	I'll come too. Nobody will stop you if I'm with you. Goodbye, Humpty. You'd better not hang about either; they're going to try to put you together again, but thank you for helping. (Kisses him.) Come on then, to the Gipsy Camp! (They run off R. HUMPTY has remained stock still and pop-eyed since being kissed.)
HUMPTY	She - she - she kissed me! Ooh, I think I'm going to fall in love. (Falls back.) Ow! Well, I've definitely fallen anyway. But I don't suppose she'll ever fall for me - unless - Yes! Now I know what to use that magic wish for when I get it. It'd be nice if I had something I could give her; something pretty and - (Sees nest-egg.) What's that? Gold eggs? Well, I could give her those. (Audience reaction as he goes to the nest-egg, which greatly surprises him. HETTY runs on from R. with a large shopping bag.)
HETTY	Oh, Humpty, naughty, naughty!
HUMPTY	Are they yours? Sorry.
HETTY	Never mind, I'll forgive you. I've been looking for you actually. I want to make sure you didn't hurt yourself falling off that wall. You see I know about these things, because I used to be a nursemaid.
MUSICAL DIRECTOR	A nursemaid?
HETTY	Relax, dear. It's much later on the surprising bit. (To HUMPTY.) Yes, a nursemaid. And one of my little charges had a very nasty fall. Little boy

	called Jack, had a sister called Jill. Well, I used vinegar and brown paper on him and it worked a treat. (Produces large sheet of brown paper from bag and starts to unfold it.)
	(RANK and FILE enter L. in their shirtsleeves carrying some pieces of broken shell. RANK has a large glue-pot and brush and FILE a tiny tub of Gripfix.)
RANK	Ah, Miss 'Encake. Excuse us, we got to put Humpty Dumpty together.
HUMPTY	But I don't want to be put together. I don't feel apart.
HETTY	And I'm just treating him for his fall with this brown paper.
RANK	File can give you a 'and then. It'll make a very good base to stick the egg shell on.
	(FILE helps HETTY wrap up HUMPTY so that only his head is showing.)
HETTY	Next year I'll remember to post you early for Christmas. Now, a little sprinkle of vinegar. (Takes vinegar bottle from bag and sprinkles HUMPTY's head with it.)
FILE	How about a little salt, too?
RANK	This ain't no time for levity, File. We got to get on with the sticking bit now. It won't be no good, but you can 'ave a go with your potty little pot of paste.
FILE	There's no need to be rude about my little potty – I mean, pot. It's jolly good stuff. I'll show you.
RANK	And I'll show you.
	(Both apply their preferred adhesives to a piece of shell, which they then stick on the brown paper. Both pieces immediately fall off.)
HETTY	Oh, very good.
RANK	Well – mine stayed on longer.
FILE	It didn't – mine did!

HUMPTY DUMPTY 47

RANK — It didn't!

FILE — It did!

RANK — (sloshing FILE with his glue brush) Didn't!

FILE — (put-out but retaliating with a tiny dab of paste on the end of RANK's nose) Did!

HETTY — (moving to them) Boys, boys, boys!

RANK — Stand back!

(He emphasises his words by moving his hand back, unfortunately the one with the glue brush in it and it lands slap in her face.)

Oh, sorry.

(She staggers back, HUMPTY shrinks his head down out of sight and FILE takes advantage of the diversion to put a rather more elaborate dab on RANK's face.

HETTY's stagger takes her in front of DOT's stall just as DOT decides to come out and see what the rumpus is about. The door opening knocks HETTY in the back to just beyond CARRYONE's stall. At which moment CARRYONE also decides to come out and knocks HETTY in the face sending her reeling back. She clutches on to the Dungeon stall door for support as she goes and pulls it open before she falls.

RANK and FILE have continued attacking each other. HUMPTY now bursts out of his paper casing and is beating a hasty retreat to R. when he is faced by the KING who enters there.

KING — Stop!

(HUMPTY does and RANK and FILE stop fighting.)

RANK — Your Majesty! (Salutes smartly, but the glue brush is in his R. hand and he sloshes himself in the face.)

KING — What's going on here? Why haven't you put - er - Hickety Pickety, no, Hickory Dickory - Humpty Dumpty together? And where's whatsisname -

48 HUMPTY DUMPTY Sc. 3

       thingummybob - the prisoner?

RANK   The prisoner, sir? (Sees open door.)
       Escaped! Somebody's filed the padlock with a file!

FILE   (reflectively) That rings a bell.

       (HETTY staggers to her feet.)

KING   And what have you been doing to Miss Cattlecake - Hencake?

RANK   Miss 'Encake? Nothing, sir.

HETTY   You did - you sloshed me with a glue brush.

RANK   Ah, that was inadvertent.

HETTY   It wasn't, it was in my face.

KING   Sergeant, this is very bad. The honour of the Army is at stake. There's a blot on your escutcheon.

RANK   Yes, sir. (Looks down at himself.) I expect it's glue, sir.

KING   No, no, no, on your - well, whatever I just said. You must wipe it off by recapturing the prisoner and driving off the rest of the gipsies. And do it with a bit of style. Ride out on those magnificent beasts -

       (HORSES look at each other and DOT laughs her neighing laugh.)

       <u>March</u> out on your magnificent feet.

       (HORSES take umbrage and run off R.)

       With your arms swinging, your accoutrements glistening, your banners flying and above all with the stirring sound of your military band!

RANK   Yes, <u>sir!</u>

FILE   But we haven't got a military band.

KING   Then form one. I'll join it myself. I've always wanted to be in a military band.

HETTY   Oh, so have I!

HUMPTY And me!

FILE   It would be rather fun.

HUMPTY DUMPTY 49

MUSIC 25 PLAY WITH ABANDON

ALL — When I was a kid it was my intent
To play a big band instrument.

KING — And if I should ever have my way
It's the trumpet I would like to play.
(Mimes playing trumpet.)

ALL — When I was a kid, etc.

HETTY — And the instrument I'd like to own
Is the big and brassy bass trombone.

(HETTY mimes playing trombone.
KING mimes playing trumpet.)

ALL — When I was a kid, etc.

RANK — I am not so fond of tum-te-tum --
I would like to bash a big bass drum.

(RANK mimes banging drum.
HETTY mimes trombone.
KING mimes trumpet.)

ALL — When I was a kid, etc.

FILE — But of all the instruments I know
It's the horn that is the thing to blow.

(FILE mimes playing horn.
RANK mimes banging drum.
HETTY mimes trombone.
KING mimes trumpet.)

ALL — When I was a kid, etc.

HUMPTY — If you ask me the sound that I prefer,
It is tuba or not tuba.

(HUMPTY mimes playing tuba.
FILE mimes horn.
RANK mimes drum.
HETTY mimes trombone.
KING mimes trumpet.)

ALL — When I was a kid it was my intent
To play a big band instrument.

(During number they move D. S. Close tabs behind them and fly in Scene 4 cloth.)

HUMPTY DUMPTY Sc. 4

Scene Four: On The Way To Somewhere

Frontcloth of exterior scene.
Open traverse tabs to reveal cloth as ALL exit R.
at end of Cumulative Number, except HUMPTY who
is going off last and who is stopped by the sound of
CHICKWEED's voice.

CHICKWEED (off L.) Mr Fowlpest! Mr Fowlpest! (She staggers on not seeing HUMPTY.) Oh dear, I've lost him. And I'm worn out searching for the end of the Rainbow; in fact, I feel –

HUMPTY Hullo.

CHICKWEED I feel great! Marvellous! Fantastic! (Spinning round.) Wheeeee!

HUMPTY I wish I could feel all that, especially the twiddly bit.

CHICKWEED It's easy. (Spinning.) Wheee! Try it.

HUMPTY Me? Twiddle? Well, why not. It could be the start of a whole new career. (Starts to twirl.) Whee-ooh-aahh!

(He gets out of control and lands in a heap. CHICKWEED runs to him.)

No, maybe not.

CHICKWEED Are you all right?

HUMPTY Not quite. I came down a nasty wallop on my Christmas pud.

CHICKWEED On your what?

HUMPTY A little snack I brought along for emergencies. Ooh! I'm sorry I left the sprig of holly on, though. (Brings from back pocket a round disc of a Christmas pudding with a sprig of holly on it.) Hm, looks more like a Christmas biccy, now.

CHICKWEED Oh, poor Humpty, shall I magic you a new one?

HUMPTY No, it's very odd, but for once I don't feel hungry. (Sighs heavily.) Perhaps it's being in love.

CHICKWEED In love? Oh, gosh! Oh, golly! Oh, Humpty!!

HUMPTY DUMPTY

	Are you really?
HUMPTY	I'm not sure. I've never been in love so I don't know what it's like. Do you?
CHICKWEED	Ooh, yes - exactly!

MUSIC 26 IT MUST BE LOVE

HUMPTY	I think I'm sickening for something bad. I must be going just a little mad. I've pains in places that I never had - It must be love.
CHICKWEED	My temper's getting in an awful state; The bathroom scales tell me I'm losing weight; I've got no interest in chocolate - It must be love.
HUMPTY	My temp'rature is rising; Romantic ballads I sing; It's really not surprising That I worry me.
CHICKWEED	My pulse is far from static; My diction is erratic, And all is symptomatic Of my malady.
HUMPTY	I feel inadequate and unrehearsed.
CHICKWEED	I meant to say it, but you said it first.
BOTH	I feel so happy I would like to burst - It must be love.

(Dance.)

HUMPTY	My life is in suspension; I'm full of nervous tension. I wouldn't care to mention All the things I dream.
CHICKWEED	I find I'm sitting staring; I don't know what I'm wearing. I'll have to get a bearing - I'm away off beam.
HUMPTY	My eyes are popping and my face is puce.
CHICKWEED	I burst out singing at the least excuse.

HUMPTY DUMPTY Sc. 4

BOTH I've tried to cure myself, but what's the use –
It must be love.
It must, it must, it must be love.

CHICKWEED (leaning forward, ready to be kissed)   Oh, Humpty!

HUMPTY The only thing is, do you think the Princess loves me?

(She looks at him for a moment, then bursts into tears and runs off R.)

Funny. I wonder if it was something I said?

FOWLPEST (off L.)   Chickweed! Chickweed!   (He enters practically on his knees.)

HUMPTY Hullo. You've just missed her.

FOWLPEST (groans)   Then I'll probably die, she's got the corn plasters and my feet are killing me. My boy, you'll never know how I've sacrificed myself trying to find the end of the Rainbow for you. I've been up hill and down dale, through town and village, field and farm, out on the heath and deep in the forest, up hill and down dale –

HUMPTY I think you said that.

FOWLPEST Well – there were two hills and two dales. But on and on I struggled, through pouring rain, 'neath broiling sun, and then more rain, and then more sun, more rain, more sun, rain, sun, rain, sun – it went on like that all the time.

HUMPTY Ah, pity you couldn't have made them happen together.

FOWLPEST Couldn't? Of course I could if I'd wanted to. But why should I want to?

HUMPTY Well, you know, if the sun's shining while the rain's falling you get a rainbow.

FOWLPEST Eh? Um. Yes. Yes, you're quite right, that *is* how you get a rainbow, but I didn't do it because – er – because you weren't with me – up all those hills and down all those dales. But now I will make a rainbow. Little bit of sun, little bit of rain,

easy! Watch.   (Starts making passes at the sky.)
Let the sun shine extra bright
Summoned by my extremely powerful wizard's might!

(LIGHTS DIM considerably. Effect 2 Thunder Roll.)

Hm. Passing cloud. Handy really, I'll use it to get the rain.   (Makes more passes skywards.)
Let the rain fall on the ground -
But don't go mad or we'll all be drown'd.

(Snow lantern starts. (If snow lantern is not used, throw on crumbled pieces of polystyrene.))

MUSIC 27

Stop!

(Snow lantern stops.)

Is it too much to ask for, pray,
A normal English summer's day?

(LIGHTS UP. Start rain lantern. (If rain lantern is not used throw on grains of rice.))

MUSIC 28 Intro and SPECTRUM BALLET

Aha! Success! Soon ev'ry shade
That forms a rainbow will be made.
And that this wonder may begin
Behold! I summon Harlequin!

(BLACKOUT. Flash R. HUMPTY and FOWLPEST exit, start to fly cloth. BRING UP SINGLE SPOT R. revealing HARLEQUIN. FADE UP remainder of lighting when cloth is clear.)

Scene Five: The End Of The Rainbow

Very open white fullset with some glitter to break it up. Cut-out ground row in front of the cyclorama. White wings L. and R.

SPECTRUM BALLET, led by HARLEQUIN who summons the various colours. A strip of red light springs up on the stage and one of the CHORUS in a red costume enters to start the ballet. A strip of orange light then springs up beside the red light followed by yellow, green, blue, indigo and violet strips, each light being accompanied by DANCERS appropriately costumed. As the ballet develops a <u>Harlequin Strobe Lantern</u> plays on the cyclorama till the ballet ends and it is then taken out, but the seven coloured strips of light remain. (A whirling colour wheel can be used instead of the <u>Harlequin Lantern</u> or the effect omitted altogether.)
<u>Swanee whistle.</u>

FOWLPEST (off L.) Woooh!

(<u>Whistle</u> ends with a <u>drum bonk</u>.)

(Off L.) Ow!

(Second <u>whistle</u> starts.)

HUMPTY (off L.) Waaah!

(<u>Whistle</u> ends with second heavier <u>bonk</u>.)

(Off L.) Ouch!

(FOWLPEST and HUMPTY enter L., rubbing their behinds.)

FOWLPEST There you see, just slide down the rainbow and you find the end of it.

HUMPTY I certainly found the end of something.

FOWLPEST Never mind, my boy. We're here now and here's your wish. (Takes it out of pocket.)
And what you ought to wish for is -

<u>MUSIC 29</u>

(ALBUMENIA hurtles on from R. on her broom-

HUMPTY DUMPTY

          stick. Screech of brakes as she pulls up.)

ALBUMENIA   Hold wizard vile! Desist! Forfend!
You slimy schemer!

HUMPTY   Who's your friend?

ALBUMENIA   One who his horrid hopes will ditch.

FOWLPEST   You would, you interfering - witch.

ALBUMENIA   Enough! No further words I'll banter.
I charge you, drop your plans instanter!

FOWLPEST   And if I don't?

ALBUMENIA   Well, then, of course,
I'll happily resort to force!

    (Buffets FOWLPEST in stomach with broomstick, causing the 'wish' to fly out of his hands and she bats it off L. with her broomstick.)

    Now that should bring your plot to naught.

CHICKWEED   (off L.)   Hey, Mr Fowlpest!   (Enters with 'wish'.)   Look!

FOWLPEST   Well caught!
How's that? You're out! And for a duck!

ALBUMENIA   A pure example of bad luck.
And though these seem such poor beginnings,
Just wait until my second innings!
(Stalks off R.)

FOWLPEST   Ha-ha! Silly old bat! Silly old bat? Oh, I'm witty with it. But now Humpty, at last my dearest dream - I mean, your dearest dream - can come true. And what is it you want, my boy? I know!

    (Making mesmeric passes at HUMPTY who stares at him apparently bemused.)

    You're aiming high, aren't you? Very high. The highest in the land. You want to be king, don't you? You want to wish - for the crown!

HUMPTY   No.

FOWLPEST   Aha! I knew - what? No?

HUMPTY	No. I want to use it to win the Princess.
	(CHICKWEED lets out a howl.)
FOWLPEST	Chickweed, stop that beastly bawling.
CHICKWEED	No, I won't! I won't, I won't, I won't!
FOWLPEST	Chickweed!
CHICKWEED	I'm sorry, Mr Fowlpest, but if that's how Humpty wants to use his wish, I won't give it to him - ever. (Puts 'wish' down front of dress.)
FOWLPEST	What! (Making to grab it from its hiding place.) Give me -
	(CHICKWEED, slightly shocked, crosses her hands protectively over herself. FOWLPEST decides on a different tack.)
	Look, be reasonable. Now, it *might* be a very good thing for Humpty to marry the Princess.
	(CHICKWEED opens her mouth to howl.)
	BUT - it's much more important for Humpty to become King. So if he promises to use the wish for that, you'll give it to him, won't you?
CHICKWEED	(reluctantly) Yes.
FOWLPEST	Then hand it over, that's what he'll do.
	(CHICKWEED puts a hand to do so.)
HUMPTY	Oh no, I -
FOWLPEST	(in a heavy aside) Shut up, you fool! Once you're King you can marry anybody you like.
CHICKWEED	I heard that, Mr Fowlpest, and now I won't give it to him whatever he promises.
FOWLPEST	Chickweed, my little weedy chick, what's come over you? Please, give him the wish and you can have anything you want. I haven't got much by me at the moment, but - Ah, how about half a dozen gold eggs to be going on with?
	(He moves to the nest-egg. The reaction sends him running back to a position between HUMPTY and

	CHICKWEED, while HETTY runs on L. so fast that she cannons into CHICKWEED so that the four of them are squashed up like sardines, facing R.)
HUMPTY) FOWLPEST) CHICKWEED) HETTY)	Ow!
	(The KING follows on immediately behind HETTY and bangs into her.)
HUMPTY) FOWLPEST) CHICKWEED) HETTY) KING)	Ow!!
	(RANK is immediately behind KING and bumps into him.)
HUMPTY) FOWLPEST) CHICKWEED) HETTY) KING) RANK)	Ow!!!
HETTY	Is this what they call a crash slimming course?
	(FILE runs on and bumps into RANK.)
ALL	Ow!!!!
	(Loud pop as the 'wish' is apparently squeezed out of the front of CHICKWEED's dress and Swanee whistle as it arches over FOWLPEST and HUMPTY. (HETTY has brought on a second blue ball and thrown it out with her U.S. hand.))
ALL FOWLPEST	(together) Ooh! The wish!
	(HUMPTY catches it.)
FOWLPEST	Aha! Quick! Wish for the crown!
KING	What? No! Stop him!
HUMPTY	But I don't want the crown. All I want is to marry

	the Princess.
KING	Marry my daughter? Certainly not. I mean, what's your background? Where do you come from?
HUMPTY	An egg.
KING	There you are. An egg. I've heard of a handbag but this is ridiculous. I'm sorry to be so <u>earnest</u>, but that sort of thing makes me <u>wild.</u>
HETTY	Well done! You deserve an Oscar for that bit.
FOWLPEST	I tell you, there's only one thing for it.
HUMPTY	I think you're right. I wish –
	(KING clutches the crown on his head with both hands.)
CHICKWEED	Oh, Humpty!
HETTY) KING) RANK) FILE)	No, Humpty!
FOWLPEST	Yes, Humpty!
HUMPTY	I wish for the crown!
	(FLASH. Cymbal crash.)
	<u>MUSIC 30</u>
	(<u>Flicker lights.</u> Enter HARLEQUIN R. ALL stand transfixed as he moves behind them and transfers the crown to HUMPTY's head, then exits L. <u>Stop flicker.</u>)
FOWLPEST	At last! At last my son is King!
HETTY) KING) RANK) FILE) CHICKWEED)	Your son?
KING	Enough of this nonsense. Army, arrest him!
FOWLPEST	No, Army! Arrest <u>Mr</u> Addlepate!

HUMPTY DUMPTY

KING Me? But I'm the King. I'm Addlepate the Dozenth.

FOWLPEST You're Addlepate the nothing. Arrest him, I say, in the name of King Humpty!

ALBUMENIA (off R.)   And I say don't!

FOWLPEST   Who's that?

ALBUMENIA (off R.)   You'll see!

(Drum roll, Flicker Lights, cymbal crash. FOWLPEST is immediately struck into an awkward crabbed position from which he is evidently unable to move.)

FOWLPEST Curses! I'm stuck!

(Second cymbal crash. CHICKWEED is similarly affected.)

CHICKWEED   And me!

(Third cymbal crash. HUMPTY cops it.)

HUMPTY   And me!

ALL THREE What's happened?

(Enter ALBUMENIA R.)

ALBUMENIA   Ah! I've cast on you
A special spell - it's laced with glue.
It doesn't last long though, and so
You four had better swiftly go.
To where you're safe is quite a tramp.

(She herds them to R.)

KING Where is it then?

ALBUMENIA   The Gipsy Camp!

KING But wait - my crown -

ALBUMENIA   Not now, away!
You'll fight for that another day.

(Pushes him off R. To RANK and FILE.)

To fight he'll need you two at hand.

RANK (salutes)   I'll smarten up this Gipsy band.
(He marches smartly off R.)

FILE	But mother said I never should Play with the gipsies in the wood.
HETTY	Mine said the same in such affairs, But now I've got the chance - who cares!
	(Pushes FILE off and exits R. herself.)
ALBUMENIA	Well, now your plans have come unstuck P'raps you will too - if you're in luck!
	(Exits R. jubilantly. <u>Ratchet.</u> FOWLPEST moves jerkily and frees himself.)
FOWLPEST	Ah!
	(Second <u>ratchet.</u> CHICKWEED does likewise.)
CHICKWEED	Ah!
	(Third <u>ratchet.</u> HUMPTY does also.)
HUMPTY	Ah!
FOWLPEST	Curse the silly old frumpface! But I'll deal with her later, and all those others. I don't like the sound of gipsies though, that could mean - well, never mind. At last my son is King! So now, my boy, for your royal enthronement. Come Rainbow Spirits! Orb and sceptre bring, And ermine robe and royal throne and ring, To make the noble Humpty Dumpty - King!
	<u>MUSIC 31</u> CORTEGG
	(A triumphant processional march led by HARLEQUIN. The RAINBOW SPIRITS bring on an ermine-tipped robe which they place on HUMPTY's shoulders, a ring which is put on his finger, an orb and sceptre which they present to him and a throne which they lead him to. As he seats himself, CHICKWEED catches his eye, then turns disconsolately away and exits. The RAINBOW SPIRITS kneel before HUMPTY. FOWLPEST is triumphant, even though HUMPTY looks an unlikely and uncomfortable monarch.)
	CURTAIN

HUMPTY DUMPTY   61

    MUSIC 32 HENTRACTE

    PART TWO

    Scene Six : The Gipsy Camp

Fullset. A woodland setting. Suitable cut-out backing and tree wings L. and R. U.C. is a large cauldron over a camp fire. D.R. is a tree stump. L. is the cut-out back of a Gipsy Caravan with steps coming down from its doorway.

    MUSIC 33 EGGUIDILLAS

    The curtain rises on a stage aswirl with the gaily coloured costumes of the CHORUS as Gipsies as they dance the lively opening number watched by ROMANO and EGLANTINE. A strangled wail is heard and the KING enters R, dressed as a gipsy. It is his attempt to join in the Flamenco spirit. The door of the caravan is flung open to reveal HETTY in an outrageous tight-bottomed and befrilled dress. She descends the steps dramatically and joins the KING for a comic dance enlivened by such mishaps as the KING becoming entangled in her shawl and their castanets getting locked together. DOT and CARRYONE enter and join in, but their hooves in the stamping routines prove something of a hazard until the CHORUS take over to bring the number to a rousing finish. Two of the CHORUS lead the HORSES away and the rest stroll off during the dialogue. The KING sinks exhausted on to the tree stump.

HETTY	Ooh! I've gone and overdone the gallivanting. In fact, my gallis never been so vanted before.
	(PRINCESS laughs and helps a very groggy HETTY up caravan steps and they exit.)
KING	Ooh! I wonder why they say horseshoes are lucky?
ROMANO	Well, aren't they?
KING	Not when the horses are still wearing them, they're not. (Rises.) Still, I suppose I'd better try and hobble home. (Moves R.)

HUMPTY DUMPTY   Sc. 6

ROMANO   But, your Majesty, you are at home.

KING   (stopping)   Really? That was quick. I'd hardly taken a - Oh, you mean here? Of course, I'm in exile, aren't I? Funny I should forget because this healthy outdoor life's been so good for my - er, my - er -

ROMANO   Memory?

KING   That's the thing. You've probably noticed how much better it is.

ROMANO   Oh - er - <u>yes</u>. So I expect you remember all about my plan to get your crown back.

KING   Oh, have you got a plan for that? So have I - Listen.

(FOWLPEST leans on from behind wing D.R. with a hand cupped to his ear.)

FOWLPEST   (sotto voce)   I shall! He-he!

CHICKWEED (appearing behind him, sotto voce)   Mr Fowlpest, they'll see you!

(She pulls him out of sight.)

KING   My plan is to send Rank and File on a spying mission to the Palace to find out where Humpty keeps the crown when he's asleep -

ROMANO   But that's -

KING   No, don't interrupt, I might forget something. Now, once we know where to find the crown just one person can steal into the Palace tonight and get it back.

ROMANO   Yes, but -

KING   But which one you're going to ask. I've thought of that, too. We'll draw lots - you, me, Hetty and Rank and File but they want to work as a team, so we'll draw lots from four bits of paper. One bit of paper will be marked with a cross, so whoever draws that gets the crown back. There - a simple little scheme, eh? Now, what was your plan?

ROMANO   That was my plan.

KING	Eh? Oh.
ROMANO	In fact, I've already sent Rank and File on their spying mission. They should be back any time now.
KING	I never knew gipsies were so efficient. Or so kind – I don't know what we'd have done without the help all of you have given us.
ROMANO	Well, gipsies are always ready to help those in trouble. They certainly helped me. You see, I'm not really a gipsy, somebody just left me with them as a baby.
KING	What?
FOWLPEST	(looking on, sotto voce) What!
CHICKWEED	(pulling him away) Ssh!
KING	Then perhaps – Hm, I wonder.
FOWLPEST	(looking on, sotto voce) So do I!
CHICKWEED	(pulling him back) Mr Fowlpest!
ROMANO	Anyway, it'll soon be sunset. I must go and see that the lookouts are ready.
KING	Then I'll go and deal with the really important part of my plan, your plan – _our_ plan.
ROMANO	What's that?
KING	Putting the cross on one of the bits of paper, of course.
	(They exit L. FOWLPEST comes on from R. followed by CHICKWEED.)
FOWLPEST	Gipsies! I said that might mean trouble. But it's my own fault, I was too kind. I should have – yes, definitely I should have.
CHICKWEED	Should have what, Mr Fowlpest?
FOWLPEST	Never mind. I shall now. Yes, I shall deal with Romano once for all. And that drawing lots business has given me an idea of how to ensnare not only him but the other four as well. There's only one snag – it doesn't include the Princess.

HUMPTY DUMPTY   Sc. 6

CHICKWEED   Oh, good!

FOWLPEST   No, it is not good. I want Humpty to marry her. So, while I fix the others, you must overcome the Princess and bring her to the Palace.

CHICKWEED   Me? Oh, dear. Oh well. But how?

FOWLPEST   Ah! With one of these new tranquillizer spells I bought recently.   (He produces from his pocket a large round disc inscribed 'SPLLE' and gives it to her.)

CHICKWEED   Why's it called 'Splle'?   (Pronounced 'splee'.)

FOWLPEST   Splle? Tt, tt. This modern workmanship. Obviously a dud. What's the good of a spell that can't spell?   (Tosses it into cauldron and produces another correctly spelt from his pocket.) Ah, that's better.

CHICKWEED   How do you use it?

FOWLPEST   Simple. Just touch her with it, say the magic words printed on the back and bingo! It happens. Now we'll hide nearby while we're waiting. This way.

(They start to go off U.L.)

1st GIPSY   (off L.)   Come on then.

2nd GIPSY   (off L.)   Coming.

FOWLPEST   Not this way! Over there!

(They run off D.R. The two GIPSIES (male) enter U.L.)

1st GIPSY   Remember, Romano said if we see anybody suspicious-looking to take them to him.

(They exit D.L.)

MUSIC 34

(RANK's head peers out from behind wing U.R., largely concealed by a big floppy black hat and a long black cloak he is holding up with his L. arm to hide his face. He lowers the cloak a little to observe briefly then raises it again as if performing

	drill movements.)
RANK	(heavy whisper) Royal spies - quick creep!
	(He creep marches on followed by FILE, who is similarly attired, but with a hat even bigger and floppier which comes down over his eyes.)
	Royal spies - freeze!
	(They stop in C.)
	Hobserve - front!
	(They turn R. to face front lower their L. arms to observe and raise them again.)
	Hobserve - rear!
	(They turn U.S. and reveal large white numbers on the back of their cloaks: 007 for RANK and $006\frac{1}{2}$ for FILE.)
	Fall out!
	(They turn to face front again.)
	The coast is clear.
FILE	Really? I didn't know you could see the sea from here. Not that I can see anything much in this hat. Do we have to wear all this?
RANK	Of course we do. This is regulation spies' uniform, this is.
FILE	But what's the point of it?
RANK	To make us hinconspicuous, of course. (Looks off L.) Look out, somebody coming!
FILE	But they're gipsies, they're on our side.
RANK	I know, but until we've reported to 'Is Majesty we're still on our mission. (In hoarse whisper.) Act unsuspicious like me and they won't notice us.
	(He puts his cloak up again to hide his face and slinks away D.R. FILE shrugs and copies but trips over his cloak and bumps into RANK.
FILE	(whispering) Sorry.

HUMPTY DUMPTY Sc. 6

(The two GIPSIES enter U.L. They stop, exchange looks, then draw daggers from their belts and creep towards RANK and FILE.)

RANK (whispering) See, they haven't noticed us.

(The GIPSIES grab them and hold the daggers to their throats.)

RANK & FILE Ow!

RANK It's all right. I think they just want to give us a shave.

1st GIPSY Silence, dogs!

FILE No, they don't. They think we're dogs.

2nd GIPSY He said, silence, dog!

FILE Sorry. I mean woof-woof.   (Pants heavily like a dog.)

(GIPSIES drag them off L. FOWLPEST looks on D.R., then enters.)

FOWLPEST Psst!

(CHICKWEED comes on.)

Nobody about. Now's your chance.

CHICKWEED (sighs) Yes, all right, Mr Fowlpest.

(He exits D.R.)

MUSIC 35

(She crosses to caravan, knocks on door and runs to hide above caravan. The door opens and HETTY appears. CHICKWEED creeps out.)

HETTY I'm here!

CHICKWEED (aside) Oh dear.   (She gets behind caravan again.)

HETTY Oh, nobody.   (Sighs.)   I thought at last one of those lovely gipsies was going to ask me to play in the woods.   (Goes back into caravan.)

CHICKWEED That's an idea.   (Running across to R.)   Mr Fowlpest!

FOWLPEST	(looking on D. R.) What is it?
	(She whispers briefly in his ear.)
	What? Certainly not.
	(She whispers more urgently and motions to caravan.)
	Oh, very well. (Goes off D. R.)
	<u>MUSIC 36</u>
	(CHICKWEED runs back to caravan, taps on door and hides above it again. HETTY comes out.)
HETTY	I think somebody's having me on. Who's there?
FOWLPEST	(puts head on D. R., wearing a gipsy headscarf. In assumed voice) Pedro. I'm lovesick and tipsy. I mean a gipsy.
HETTY	At last! What do you want?
FOWLPEST	Come and play in the woods.
HETTY	(running down steps) Oh, yes, yes, yes! (Stops.) Oh, no, no, no. Do you promise not to trifle with my girlish affections?
FOWLPEST	Yes!
HETTY	And do you promise not to take advantage of my innocence?
FOWLPEST	Yes!!
HETTY	And not to try for a bit of slap and tickle when I'm not looking?
FOWLPEST	Yes!!!
HETTY	Hardly worth coming then.
FOWLPEST	Oh, please come and play in the woods.
HETTY	Oh, very well. What shall we play?
FOWLPEST	(aside) I hadn't thought of that. (In assumed voice.) Er - dominoes. (Disappears.)
HETTY	Dominoes? (Shrugs.) All right, but I warn you I'll knock spots off you!
	(Runs off R. CHICKWEED registers relief and

	goes to knock on door again, but the PRINCESS opens it. She remains standing in the doorway to CHICKWEED's frustration.)
PRINCESS	(laughing) Hetty's found herself a gipsy at last. I wonder where my gipsy is? I think Daddy might let me marry him now, unless he's worried because he can't give me a dowry.
	(Comes down steps and moves D. S. to CHICKWEED's relief. She starts creeping after her.)
	We haven't got anything now, not so much as a single gold egg.
	(CHICKWEED is just about to pounce as the PRINCESS sees the nest-egg moves to it.)
	What's this? Gold eggs!
	(The reaction sends CHICKWEED scuttling off behind the caravan and HETTY runs on R.)
HETTY	Who is it? Who's the naughty - Oh, it's you. I'm afraid that's the privy nest-egg, dear. All these nice people look after it for me.
PRINCESS	(going up steps) Oh, I'm sorry, and I've called you away from your gipsy.
HETTY	Never mind, dear, I don't think he was really my type. Too athletic.
PRINCESS	Too athletic?
HETTY	Yes, he ran away too fast.
	(PRINCESS exits into caravan and HETTY is about to follow as ROMANO enters U. L. Start SLOW FADE to romantic evening light.)
ROMANO	Ah, Hetty, I hoped you'd be alone.
HETTY	Oh, Romano, this is so sudden. I'm yours!
ROMANO	I mean alone without the Princess so we can do the draw. But we're wondering what's happened to Rank and File.
1st GIPSY	(off L.) Come on, move!
	(He thrusts RANK on at dagger-point.)

RANK	Ow! You shoved that right in my –
	(GIPSY jabs his behind with dagger.)
	Ow! You shoved it there again.
1st GIPSY	Two spies, Romano.
ROMANO	(laughing) Two spies?
1st GIPSY	Yes, the other one's mad.
	(FILE enters on all fours barking loudly, followed by the 2nd GIPSY.)
FILE	You see, it's all right if you –
	(2nd GIPSY prods him in behind with dagger.)
	Ow! That's no way to treat even a dog. (Rises.)
ROMANO	I think there's been a slight mistake. They're not spies –
RANK	No, of course we're not.
FILE	Yes, we are. You said so.
	(The two GIPSIES grab them round their necks.)
RANK	All right, we're spies, but we're goody spies not baddy spies.
ROMANO	They've been spying for us. Don't worry, they're all right.
	(GIPSIES release them.)
	I'm glad you're so alert though.
1st GIPSY	Well, we always keep a good look-out, Romano.
	(They exit D.L.)
HETTY	Funny – I wonder why they've missed me then?
	(KING enters U.L., carrying a hat with pieces of paper in it.)
KING	Here we are, everything's ready for the draw. Oh, you're back. Any luck?
RANK	(saluting smartly) Yes, sir! Mission successful, sir! We 'ave discovered the location of the crown at night, sir. 'Umpty Dumpty keeps it in his bedroom,

	sir, which is the Blue Room in the West Wing, sir.
	<u>MUSIC 37</u>
KING	The Blue Room!
HETTY	In the West Wing. But that's –
BOTH	The Haunted Bedroom!
RANK	Yes, but it's also the only bedroom what 'as a safe in it, sir. And that's where he puts the crown.
ROMANO	A safe! What's the combination?
KING	The combination? It's – er – as it was for me I know I told them to make it easy – Oh yes, of course. 1 2 3 – er
ROMANO	Four?
KING	That's it! How did you guess? Anyway, now we can get on with the draw.
	(FOWLPEST looks on U. R.)
FOWLPEST	(sotto voce) Aha! Just in time. Now to fix it. He-he! (Tiptoes across to hide behind cauldron.) There'll be one cross so I'll make three more. (Produces trick card with three large crosses on it.)
KING	(places hat on tree stump) All ready?
HETTY	No, wait, as it's the Haunted Bedroom, I think whoever draws the paper with the cross should go disguised as a ghost.
OTHERS	Yes, good idea.
FOWLPEST	(smiling, aside) Very!
ROMANO	And let's make it a secret draw. Then whoever is chosen can just slip quietly away.
OTHERS	Agreed.
KING	Right, now all draw together.
	(As they move their hands to the hat FOWLPEST passes his across the card and the crosses disappear apparently into his fist from which he seemingly throws them into the hat. (See 'Special Instructions.'))

MUSIC 38

(Sting. The others each draw out a piece of paper. RANK draws for his team.)

ROMANO (unfolds his paper and reveals the cross on it. Smiles) Well, there's - one or two things I must go and do. (Exit L.)

KING (unfolds his paper and also reveals cross. Agitatedly) Yes, come to think of it, there's one or two things I must go and do. (Exit L.)

HETTY (opens her paper and reveals cross. Gives an hysterical giggle) Well, isn't that a coincidence? There's one or two things I must go and do. (Exit L.)

RANK (opens paper) There's one or two things we must go and do, too.

FILE Are there?

RANK Yes.

(He shows FILE the cross on their paper. FILE faints into his arms.)

I can see this is going to be a right drag.

(RANK hauls him off L. FOWLPEST emerges from behind cauldron.)

FOWLPEST He-he! That's certainly fixed them. I'll go and prepare a little reception for them. And I hope Chickweed hurries up and deals with the Princess. She's asleep! Chickweed!

(She emerges from behind caravan. End SLOW FADE.)

CHICKWEED What? Oh, sorry Mr Fowlpest, I was just -

FOWLPEST Get on with it. (Exit R.)

CHICKWEED (yawns) Well, it's past my bedtime. (Leans on L. side of caravan steps.) Now how can I -

(PRINCESS opens caravan door. CHICKWEED slips to L. side of caravan.)

(Aside.) That's lucky.

PRINCESS	What a lovely evening. Just the evening for something exciting to happen.
CHICKWEED	(creeping up on her) Yes!
	(KING enters L. hurriedly with a white sheet over his arm. CHICKWEED runs back to L. of caravan.)
PRINCESS	Hullo, Daddy.
KING	(startled, tries to hide sheet) Oh, hullo - I - er - I - er -
	(Starts to whistle airily and strolls to R., breaking into a run just before he gets off. CHICKWEED starts to creep out again.)
PRINCESS	I wonder what that was about?
	(HETTY enters hurriedly L., also carrying a white sheet. CHICKWEED scuttles back.)
	Well, well.
HETTY	(startled, tries to hide sheet) What! Oh - er -
	(She also whistles airily, strolls to R. and breaks into a run before going off. CHICKWEED approaches PRINCESS again.)
PRINCESS	How very peculiar. I wonder -
	(RANK and FILE enter hurriedly L., each carrying a white sheet.)
	I say -
	(RANK and FILE try to hide sheets.)
RANK	Oh, Your 'Ighness! We - er -
	(Breaks into airy whistle. FILE copies him, they stroll to R., then stop momentarily.)
	Come on!
	(He and FILE run off R. PRINCESS looks off L., to see who RANK was addressing. DOT and CARRY-ONE trot on, each with a folded white sheet on their backs. On seeing the PRINCESS they slow down and lift their heads to whistle. When they reach R. they

HUMPTY DUMPTY 73

	break into a run to exit. CHICKWEED once more creeps out.)
PRINCESS	Whoever next I wonder?
	(ROMANO enters L. carrying a white sheet. He is already whistling, but quite genuinely. CHICKWEED shrugs and exits D.L.)
	Mind if I join in?
ROMANO	(stops) Oh.
PRINCESS	No, don't stop. Let's whistle together. (Takes his hand.)
ROMANO	Whistle?
PRINCESS	Yes, you know, like this.
	(She pulls him over to R. as she whistles airily.)
	And then we suddenly start to run.
ROMANO	Do we? Why?
PRINCESS	You tell me. And what's that?
ROMANO	This? Oh. It's a sheet.
PRINCESS	I can see that. But what's it for?
ROMANO	Well - I - er - I just sort of picked it up and - and - (Decides to get rid of it and throws it off R.)
PRINCESS	And now you've thrown it down.
ROMANO	Yes. Well, I didn't really want it. But what was this whistling business?
PRINCESS	I don't know. But everybody seems to be doing it.
ROMANO	Perhaps they're just happy. Aren't you happy?
PRINCESS	Now. Very.
ROMANO	So am I. Shall we always be, do you think?
PRINCESS	You're the gipsy - you're the one who should tell fortunes.
	MUSIC 39 STARS IN YOUR EYES
ROMANO	In the palm of your hand is your destiny showing; The way of the cards is the way life is going;

74   HUMPTY DUMPTY   Sc. 6

                    A glance at the stars is a sure way of knowing
                        The road where our destiny lies.

PRINCESS   In the crystal I gazed on the face of my true love,
                        The face was my fortune, the face that was you, love.

BOTH   I've seen ev'ry sign that I'm yours and you're mine
                        In the light of the stars in your eyes.

ROMANO   Cross a palm with silver and you'll be told
                        Ev'rything you want to know.

PRINCESS   Look into the crystal and you'll behold
                        Ev'ry place that you should go.

BOTH   Symbols, signs and portents abound, my love.
                    Now at last I know that I have found my love.

ROMANO   In the palm of your hand, etc.

                    (CHORUS enter during number. Music continues
                    quietly with the CHORUS humming softly. ROMANO
                    exits R. and the PRINCESS sits dreamily on the
                    steps. CHICKWEED looks on D. L. but one of the
                    CHORUS enters U. L. with a tray of mugs and each
                    of the CHORUS takes one and dips it into the
                    cauldron.)

CHICKWEED   (aside)   This is ridiculous. Now they're going to
                    have a meal.

                    (She is just about to go when the CHORUS sip at
                    their mugs. <u>Music stops with a big music sting.</u>
                    They all flake out. PRINCESS sits up very
                    surprised. CHICKWEED whirls round.)

                    Spiles do work!

                    (PRINCESS moves U. S. to investigate.)

                    Now's my chance.   (Takes out her spell disc.)
                    Just touch her with it and read the magic words on
                    the back.   (She creeps up and touches PRINCESS
                    with the disc.)   'Made in England'!

PRINCESS   (turning)   What? Who are -

CHICKWEED   Oh no!   (Looks at disc again.)

PRINCESS)   Wait a minute - you're -
CHICKWEED)   (together)
                                Alakahocusdabra!

HUMPTY DUMPTY 75

(CHICKWEED touches PRINCESS with disc.)

MUSIC 40

(Sting. PRINCESS falls straight into her arms.)

CHICKWEED Oh dear! Oh well, it's only five miles to the Palace.

(As she struggles off with her

MUSIC 41

and

BLACKOUT.
Close traverse tabs and fly in Scene 7 cloth.)

Scene Seven : Outside The Palace

Frontcloth. Exterior setting. (Scene 4 cloth could possibly be used again.) Open traverse tabs to reveal cloth as soon as ready during scene.

MUSIC 42

ALBUMENIA enters R., despondently dragging a broomstick behind her so that it is largely concealed.

ALBUMENIA Oh really, it's beyond a jest;
Once more I've failed my flying test.
And just because I chanc'd, you see,
To bump into a beastly tree.
What's worse, besides not getting through,
I've lost my no-claim bonus too!
(She reveals the broomstick. It has a handle like a crumpled corkscrew. She sighs.)
Things really aren't too bright all round,
I doubt though if I'll gain much ground
Unless I take some action drastic,

	Something bizarre and quite fantastic. But what? Ah, yes! Oh, no. Oh dear. (Sees something off L.) Well, well - what's Chickweed doing here? (CHICKWEED enters backwards L., still pulling the inert PRINCESS.)
CHICKWEED	Phew! This tranquillizer spell has its disadvantages. I must have a little rest. (Puts PRINCESS in upright position where she remains rigid.) It's lucky she stays upright. And we're nearly there now. I just hope nobody sees us. (ALBUMENIA coughs and taps her on shoulder. She whirls round, gives a little scream and tries to lift the PRINCESS bodily.)
ALBUMENIA	Don't screech and try to run like that, But kindly tell me what you're at. And do not try the truth to fog Or in a trice you'll be a frog.
CHICKWEED	I quite like frogs.
ALBUMENIA	All right a toad!
CHICKWEED	Ooh no!
ALBUMENIA	Then why this curious load? Is it some plot of Fowlpest's hatching?
CHICKWEED	Well, yes, I'm sort of Princess snatching. Because she wasn't in the draw; The other five, they were.
ALBUMENIA	What for? It sounds so cramp'd.
CHICKWEED	No, not this kind. (Mimes opening a drawer.) I mean a draw you draw to find - Well, who is in and who is out.
ALBUMENIA	They weren't all in? Squeez'd out, no doubt.
CHICKWEED	I think you don't quite understand, This draw was <u>fix'd</u>, by sleight of hand,

HUMPTY DUMPTY

By Fowlpest.

ALBUMENIA   This gets stranger still;
You mean at woodwork he's some skill?

CHICKWEED   No, no! He'd fix'd the draw, to draw them –

ALBUMENIA   Now there's two drawers.

CHICKWEED   There's not. Ignore them.
They just don't matter, not two straws,
'Cos no one was in any drawers.

(ALBUMENIA reacts.)

Oh dear, that doesn't sound too good.
I'll start again.

ALBUMENIA   I think you should!

CHICKWEED   The others, Fowlpest – don't mind how! –
Lur'd to the Palace. Got that?

(ALBUMENIA nods, but is still puzzled.)

Now –
The Princess he – well, left to me.
So that is why we're here. You see?

ALBUMENIA   Yes, some faint notion's breaking through.
But what's the end he has in view?

CHICKWEED   To marry her, to Humpty. So
I have to help.   (Sniffs.)   Don't want to,
though.
I'd rather take her anywhere
As long as it was not – well, there.

ALBUMENIA   (striking her forehead)   Wait!

<u>MUSIC 43</u>

(A balloon shape descends over her head with
'IDEA' written on it.)

So you shall. My action drastic
Has snapp'd at me like stretch'ed elastic!
'Twill win the battle for the crown –
Take the Princess to Underdown!

(<u>Swanee whistle</u> as balloon whisks out of sight.)

CHICKWEED	The Goblin King!	
ALBUMENIA	That's right.	
CHICKWEED	Well, gosh! I think that's going too far.	
ALBUMENIA	Bosh! If you want Humpty then don't tarry. (CHICKWEED moves to PRINCESS.) Now naught shall make my plans miscarry. MUSIC 44 (Sting. PRINCESS comes out of her spell.)	
PRINCESS	I've been bewitch'd.	
CHICKWEED	Oh, dear!	
PRINCESS	(grasping her in a half-nelson) By you! The White Witch – good, she'll help me – (But ALBUMENIA makes a magic pass at her.) MUSIC 45 (Sting.) Ooh! (PRINCESS releases CHICKWEED and puts her arms straight out in front of her and gazes fixedly ahead.)	
ALBUMENIA	Sorry, Princess, no time for talking. (To CHICKWEED.) The spell I've cast is call'd sleep-walking. (PRINCESS moves forward slowly.) To Goblin Land now hurry, dear, You'll find it easy. (PRINCESS almost walks into pit. ALBUMENIA just stops her and points her to L.) If you steer.	
CHICKWEED	Yes. Right hand down then. (PRINCESS almost walks into pros. arch.)	

	I mean, left! At which is which I'm none too deft.
	(They exit L.)
ALBUMENIA	Well, now events will move apace. I'd better, though, just sweep the place. A spell can leave a residue Which other folk might walk into.
	(A GIPSY GIRL hurries on L. looking behind her.)
GIPSY GIRL	The Princess! And with –
ALBUMENIA	Stop!

(As the GIRL turns to her, still moving forward, she reaches the place where the PRINCESS was.)

MUSIC 46

(Sting and she goes into a slow walk with glazed eyes and out-stretched hands.)

       Too late.
Still, I've an idea. Yes. Just wait.

(Puts her hand up to GIRL who slowly marks time. ALBUMENIA produces a piece of paper and a quill pen.)

This slight mistake can profit earn (Writes.)
Addressed – 'To Whom It May Concern'.
Then for the message, P.T.O.

(Turns paper over, writes briefly and puts it into GIPSY GIRL's hand.)

Now to the Palace off you go.

(GIPSY GIRL sleep walks off R. ALBUMENIA sweeps busily where the spell over the PRINCESS was cast. Close traverse tabs. Fly out cloth.)

I'm sure my ploy with Underdown
Has caused your brows a worried frown,
But sometimes one must break to mend –
'Twill turn out all right in the end.

MUSIC 47

(As she exits R. BLACKOUT. Open traverse tabs.)

HUMPTY DUMPTY   Sc. 8

Scene Eight : The Haunted Bedroom

A box inset representing a bedroom in rather
gloomy blue decor. (This can be inset in Scene 6
if low flats, profiled at the top are used. The
construction of some of the tricks in this scene are
given in 'Special Instructions' at the end of the text.)
D.R. is the main door opening onstage, which is
open to begin. Above it is a wall safe, (practical
door) with a combination knob, and letters, not
figures round the dial. Over the safe is a portrait
of some ancestral gentleman whose eyes can be
moved. Across the U.R. corner is a window. U.C.
is a double bed and at the foot of it a chest – long
enough for a person to lie full length – with a
hinged lid. L. of the bed is a table with nylon lines
attached to move it. To the L. of the bed hangs a
trick picture of a sailing ship. In the L.C. back
wall is a hole, covered with a flap, to allow a blow
pipe to be put through. Across the U.L. corner is
a door opening onstage with a bathroom backing.
Below it is a built-in wardrobe cupboard with a door
opening onstage. D.L. is a secret panel, which
swivels on a vertical axis. Dim lighting to open.

The LIGHTS COME UP as HUMPTY appears in the
open doorway D.R., carrying a candlestick with a
lighted candle and a plate on which is a huge
sandwich. He is wearing a nightshirt, bedsocks and
a nightcap with the crown on top of it. Fade music.)

HUMPTY   Amazing how much light one candle gives, isn't it?
                      (Moving in.)   And just in case I feel peckish in the
                      night I've got myself a dainty little sandwich.
                      (Puts candlestick and plate on table beside bed.
                      Yawns and stretches.)   Ah, bedibyes. Oh no,
                      toothipegs.

                      (Exit through U.L. door. Brief pause. FOWLPEST
                      looks on through D.R. door.)

FOWLPEST   Humpty? Oh, not gone to bed yet.   (Enters and
                      shuts door.)   I want to warn him that the ghosts
                      coming here tonight aren't real ones. He-he!
                      They'll wish they were by the time I've done with

	them. There's a legend that this bedroom's supposed to be haunted, you see, but I started that legend years ago with a few ingenious little devices I fixed up. Things like that table moving, (Points to table.) and the eyes in that portrait moving, too. (Points to portrait.) Then there's a ghost with its head tucked underneath its arm, a skeleton and lots of groans and creaks and so on. I'll just go and check that everything's working properly. (Sees the sandwich on table and picks it up.) Tt tt, I do wish Humpty wouldn't leave food lying around, it only encourages mice. Now, there's a secret panel here somewhere. Ah, yes. (Crashes into wall L. above panel. Rubs nose.) Oh, no. (Putting out a hand to lean on wall.) Well, where on earth - ? (Leans on D. S. end of panel and almost falls through gap.) Of course.
	(He exits through the secret panel. HUMPTY returns.)
HUMPTY	Now for bed. Oh no, must put the crown away. (Moves to safe.) Luckily the combination's easy. (Turning knob.) E-A-S-Y. (Opens door and puts crown in and shuts door then turns knob again.) There. (Moves to bed and gets into it.) Ah, bed at last. They say this room's supposed to be haunted, but I don't believe it. (Lies down. Slight pause then he puts his head up again.) Pity, I just cleaned my teeth. I feel like my sandwich already.
	(Not looking he puts out his L. hand to take it. As he does so <u>Swanee whistle</u> and the table moves L. As his hand doesn't connect with the table where he expects it to be he almost topples out of bed.)
	Funny. I thought the table was nearer than that - and what's happened to my sandwich?
	(<u>Effect 3. Cackling laugh</u> sounds L. causing HUMPTY to sit bolt upright.)
	What was that? It came from over there.
	(He looks round at the portrait. <u>The eyes swivel.</u>

He claps a hand to his eyes.)

I didn't see that.

(He takes hand away. Eyes in the portrait swivel again.)

I did see that!

(Blow-pipe comes through hole and blows out candle. DIM LIGHTS.)

Aooh!

(Effect 4. Squeak as handle on D.R. door turns.)

Wh - wh - who's there?

(Effect 5. Creak as door swings open.)

Go away! You won't f - f - fr - frighten me!

(Door slams shut. (Nylon line has been attached while door was closed.)

Much!

(Effect 6. Ghastly groan off L.)

Ooh!

(Effect 7. Clank of ball and chain off L. HUMPTY gulps. Secret panel swivels slowly and GHOSTLY FIGURE with head tucked under arm emerges dragging a ball and chain on its feet. (Trick costume on one of CHORUS. See 'Special Instructions'.) Effect 8. Another groan accompanied by mouth of head opening.)

Waah!

(HUMPTY dives under the bedclothes. FIGURE disappears. Effect 9. Wind noise off R. Windows U.R. blow open. The bedclothes are flung off (by HUMPTY). Effect 10. Sound of rattling bones R. SKELETON appears in the window and dances about. HUMPTY mouths wordlessly at it. SKELETON disappears. HUMPTY screams, stumbles hastily to the door D.R. and exits. FOWLPEST re-enters through secret panel with a lighted taper. LIGHTS UP. He re-lights candle.)

FOWLPEST	Yes, yes, all working. Pity there was nobody here. Funny thing though, I don't remember putting in that scream right at the end. Still, very effective. But some of the levers were a little stiff. I'll give them a drop of oil. And I'd better find Humpty. I want him to get to bed before the others arrive.

(Exit through door R.)

MUSIC 48

(A ghostly sheeted figure looks on through the window, then enters. The figure lifts up the front of the sheet and ADDLEPATE is revealed.)

ADDLEPATE	Nobody here. Good. Then I can - er - I can - well, I must have come here for something. Really I'm not safe - safe! That's it. (Moves to safe.) And the combination's easy - just 1 2 3 4. (Sees dial.) Oh. That isn't easy. (Moving D.S.) Now what can I -

(Effect 11. Handle on door D.R. squeaks and starts to turn.)

Someone coming!

MUSIC 49

(He backs away to L. as the door opens slowly and two sheeted figures creep on. The KING stifles a cry, looks for the nearest hiding place to him and gets into the built-in wardrobe L. The new ghosts have not seen him. The 1st GHOST stops and turns to his L. The 2nd GHOST shuts the door and then backs into him. 1st GHOST springs round.)

1st GHOST	Aah! A ghost!
2nd GHOST	It's me, you fathead.
1st GHOST	S-s-sergeant Rank?
RANK	(raising sheet) Yes, of course.
1st GHOST	Oh, good. And don't be frightened. I'm Private File. (Raises sheet.)
RANK	I know that! Make a recce and see the coast's clear while I deal with the safe.

| | HUMPTY DUMPTY | Sc. 8 |

       (FILE moves round the room. RANK goes to safe.)

       1 2 3 4. That should be easy.   (Sees dial.) Oh.

FILE   Oooh, look!

RANK   (worried)   What?

FILE   Gold eggs.

RANK   Well, that's handy. Let's take 'em.

       (They move to nest-egg. Reaction, which sends them scuttling up to either side of the bed. The secret panel revolves and HETTY, covered by a sheet, whirls through it. RANK and FILE give a cry and dive under either side of the bed.)

HETTY   (raising her sheet, to Audience)   Don't worry, it's just me.   (Moving C. and looking round.) Oh dear, I've missed them - or perhaps it was a ghost, eh?   (Laughs gaily.)   Not that I really believe in ghosts, you know.

       <u>MUSIC 50</u>

       (Bathroom door opens and ROMANO, covered with a sheet, backs on.)

       Aah! I do!

       (She is at the foot of the bed so lifts the chest lid, steps into it, lies down and pulls the lid shut. ROMANO turns and raises his sheet.)

ROMANO   Ah, there's the safe. Good. But I'd better make sure nobody's outside.

       (As he moves to door D.R., it is flung open and he is caught behind it. A very fearful HUMPTY enters holding a blunderbuss in his shaking hands.)

HUMPTY   If there's any more skeletons, ghosts or anything else, I'll fill them full of lead. Well, I will when I've loaded this. I put some powder and shot in this cupboard.

       (Puts out a hand to open cupboard. ROMANO tries to come out from behind door which creaks slightly. <u>Effect 12.</u> HUMPTY turns to look, but

ROMANO has dodged back. At the same time, the
KING opens the cupboard door and puts a powder horn
and a leather shot pouch into HUMPTY's outstretched
hand.)

Thank you.

(KING shuts door. HUMPTY moves away and does a
big delayed double-take on what he is holding and the
cupboard, then loads the blunderbuss feverishly.
ROMANO starts to creep across behind him.)

I don't like it. I don't like it at all. I keep feeling
there's somebody behind me.   (Reaction.)
What? There's a ghost?   (Reaction. He gulps.)
Well, I'll look.

(Moving L. he turns right round slowly with ROMANO
following closely behind him, until he faces front
again.)

You fibbers, you're just trying to frighten me.
(Reaction.)   Well, I'll look the other way.

(Moves round to his R. and ROMANO follows closely
again.)

There's nothing.   (Reaction.)   Well, it must be
an invisible ghost.   (Reaction.)   But I've
looked both ways - round this way -

(Swings to face L., ROMANO quickly dodges behind
him.)

And this way, and there's -

(Swings so quickly round that ROMANO is caught out.)

Aah!

(Flings blunderbuss on bed and lifts the chest lid to
get into the chest. GREEN SPOT on HETTY as she
sits up slowly.)

Aaah!

(He runs to get under the bed. RANK and FILE
emerge on either side.)

Aaaah!!!

HUMPTY DUMPTY   Sc. 8

(He runs over to the wardrobe. The KING opens the door and steps out.)

Aaaaaah!!!

(HUMPTY flees over the steps at L. of stage, down into the auditorium and out through front exit door L. (The following directions, given from the actors' point of view, assume an auditorium with aisles along each side, transverse aisles front and back and exit doors L. and R. at the front and back, also a pass door to the stage through the R. front exit. Naturally a different layout will require the business to be suitably adapted.))

<u>MUSIC 51</u>

(The GHOSTS realise each other's presence and all, except ROMANO, are terrified. HETTY turns and runs over R. steps into auditorium. KING does likewise over L. steps. Both run along front transverse aisle until they meet when they turn and run back and exit through the L. and R. front exits respectively. At the same time, RANK and FILE have jumped onto the bed and collided. When they have disentangled themselves, they run out of the window. HUMPTY looks on fearfully through L. front exit door and creeps onto the stage where ROMANO moves across to him. He flees back down steps followed by ROMANO and runs along the front transverse aisle. As he gets to the R. end of it, RANK and FILE appear through the R. front exit door. HUMPTY turns and runs up R. aisle. RANK and FILE, frightened by ROMANO, follow after him and ROMANO chases after them. All stream out through R. exit at back.
<u>Music stops.</u>
FOWLPEST enters onstage with an oil can.)

FOWLPEST   Still not here? No, quiet as the grave. I'll just go and oil those levers.   (He exits through secret panel.)

(The KING enters through L. front exit, raises sheet and makes his way onto stage, and towards window.)

HUMPTY DUMPTY

KING Thank goodness they've all gone. I'll get away while there are no nasty spooks.

(Effect 13. SKELETON appears in window.)

Waah!

MUSIC 52

(SKELETON goes as KING runs to R. steps. At the same moment HETTY enters through R. front exit going towards the same steps. They scare each other. The KING turns and bolts out through D.R. door onstage. HETTY runs along the front transverse aisle just as HUMPTY bursts through the L. exit at back, followed by RANK and FILE and ROMANO, who all run down L. aisle. HETTY, seeing them, runs onto stage over L. steps and up to window. KING appears there, again they mutually frighten each other. KING disappears back through the window. HUMPTY and CO. have also come on stage over L. steps. HUMPTY breaks off to run out through bathroom door. RANK, FILE and ROMANO run off through door D.R. HETTY dithers and lands up beside the secret panel and lifts sheet. Music stops.

HETTY If I see any more ghosts I shall come over all unnecessary.

(Secret panel swings round with GHOSTLY FIGURE. She doesn't really take it in.)

Good evening.

GHOSTLY FIG. (moving mouth in carried head, in deep sepulchral tones) Good evening.

HETTY What a low voice. I suppose it's because you keep your head right down there. (Double take.) Right down there! Aah!

MUSIC 53

(Runs up and exits through window. GHOSTLY FIGURE exits through panel. HUMPTY creeps on nervously through bathroom door to L. of bed. HETTY, KING, RANK, FILE and ROMANO pour in through the window. HUMPTY grabs the

	blunderbuss and levels it at them. <u>Music stops.</u>)
OTHERS	(throwing off their sheets) Don't shoot!
	(HUMPTY lowers blunderbuss.)
ALL	(to each other) What are you doing here?
	(DOT and CARRYONE, with sheets on, gallop through bathroom door and neigh. ALL react. HUMPTY swings round and raises the blunderbuss but averts his eyes as he pulls trigger so that he moves the muzzle U.S. There is a bang. <u>Effect 14.</u> <u>(Starter pistol</u> off.) A little puff of smoke appears amidships in the ship picture, and the vessel breaks in two.
	<u>MUSIC 54</u> 'Rule Britannia'
	as it sinks slowly beneath the waves. FOWLPEST enters through secret panel.
FOWLPEST	So! I have you all in my power!
	(ROMANO steps towards him. He levels oil can at them.)
	Stay where you are or I'll drill you full of oil!
HETTY	Ah, an oil drill.
	(The GIPSY GIRL sleep-walks on through door D.R. holding ALBUMENIA's note in front of her. ROMANO takes the note and she sleep-walks off again.)
	Funny lady.
ROMANO	(reading) 'To Whom It May Concern, from a Well-Wisher.'
FILE	Oh, isn't that nice?
ROMANO	There's more. (Reading.) 'P.T.O.' (Turns over.) 'Chickweed has taken the Princess to Underdown, the King of the Goblins.'
FOWLPEST) OTHERS)	(together) Chickweed! What!
ROMANO	We must save her!
ALL	Yes, to the Land of the Goblins!

(As EVERYONE starts to run off BLACKOUT.)

MUSIC 55

(Close traverse tabs and fly in Scene 9 cloth.)

Scene Nine : On The Way To The Way Down

Frontcloth with opening cut in it. Exterior with the trunk of an old tree C. which is riven by a large cleft at its base to provide the opening. Open traverse tabs as soon as ready during scene. Hurry music continues until we hear neighing off C. and FOWLPEST enters R. mounted on CARRYONE.

FOWLPEST   Come on, Humpty, my boy!

(DOT runs on L.)

Humpty, where are you?

(HUMPTY enters L.)

HUMPTY   I fell off. It's this nightshirt. I'm not used to riding sidesaddle.

FOWLPEST   Well, we don't need to ride any further.

(CARRYONE drops his rear end and FOWLPEST falls off.)

Ow! Impatient beast. Anyway, it's lucky we took the horses. The cleft in that tree is the way down to Goblin Land. We'll find the Princess before the others.

HUMPTY   Yes.   (Sighs.)   The trouble is, though, she doesn't love me, she loves Romano.

FOWLPEST   Ah, I've thought of that.   (Produces a paper bag.) Look - magic biscuits. A mere nibble at one of 'em makes anybody dote on the next live creature that

	they see. I adapted the idea from an old Greek recipe. So just give the Princess one of these and – oh dear.

(He points at CARRYONE who has dipped his nose in the bag which HUMPTY holds in his L. hand. DOT moves in and nudges him. He looks round at her.

MUSIC 56

They execute a touching little pas de deux and exit L. on tiphoof.)

FOWLPEST — Whew! Lucky he didn't look this way. I remember there was some trouble with an ass the first time it was tried out. But they never got to the bottom of that. Anyway, let's get down below. No, don't let's. Here comes Romano. We'll lead him astray then double back.

(ROMANO runs on L.)

ROMANO — Where is it? Where's the way down?

FOWLPEST — This way. Follow us!

(They run off L. with ROMANO following.)

MUSIC 57

(ALBUMENIA enters R. on broomstick.)

ALBUMENIA —
There – all united in one cause,
All rushing hither without pause.
To make sure they find Eglantine,
I'll point the way down with a sign.
(Makes a pass at tree.)

MUSIC 58

(Sting. ILLUMINATED SIGN with a hand pointing to cleft and saying: 'TO GOBLIN LAND' appears beside tree.)

And she and Chickweed, I would judge,
Should just be there now.

(CHICKWEED enters L. gripped in a firm half-nelson by the PRINCESS.)

CHICKWEED — Help!

HUMPTY DUMPTY

ALBUMENIA: Oh, fudge! What's happened?

CHICKWEED: Somehow we went wrong, Then she woke up and ooh! She's strong.

ALBUMENIA: My spell wore off then?

PRINCESS: (grips CHICKWEED even more firmly) Yes!

CHICKWEED: You bet!

PRINCESS: But there's one thing I don't quite get — Why aren't you helping me not her?

ALBUMENIA: That question's answer —

(Shouts from RANK and FILE and KING off L.)

I'll defer! No time to talk.

(PRINCESS opens her mouth to protest.)

No, not one peep.
I charge you, dear, go off to sleep.
(Makes magic pass at her.)

MUSIC 59

(Sting. PRINCESS falls limp.)

Catch her Chickweed!

(CHICKWEED does.)

Well held! Away!

(Helps CHICKWEED to bundle PRINCESS into tree cleft.)

Somehow the others I'll delay.
(Starting to sweep.) But first I'll sweep up with all speed
In case the spell — Too late!

(KING and RANK and FILE run on L. till they reach where the PRINCESS was standing L.C.

MUSIC 60

Sting. They stop dead and fall in a snoring heap.)

No need!

HUMPTY DUMPTY   Sc. 9

Before I'd time to sweep it fully
They'd caught the residue. How bully!

(Exit R. HETTY enters L. She has a miner's helmet with Davy lamp on it and carries a coal scuttle.)

HETTY   I thought I'd better come prepared. I might be able to get a scuttle-full while I'm down below.

(RANK and FILE and KING give a loud snore each.)

Goodness! Fancy them going to sleep when we have to rescue the Princess.   (Shaking them.)
Oi, wakey-wakey! Wake up, dears! WAKE UP!
Well, I don't know. Yes I do! My little song.
That'll wake 'em!

<u>MUSIC 61</u> TOP OF THE WORLD (Reprise refrain.)

Bang, bash, clatter and crash!
  Throw yourself about.
If you whisper
  They won't hear you shout.
Bang, bash, clatter and crash!
  Keep the flag unfurled.
Bang, bash, clatter and crash!
  You'll be on top of the world.

(KING, RANK and FILE snore again.)

This is ridiculous - nobody sleeps when I'm on. They must have been bewitched. In that case, I'll do a little magic myself. Watch. I pull the invisible magic cord   (Does so.)   and say the magic words,   (Shouting up to flies.)   Oi, Fred!

(The SONG SHEET descends.)

Amazing, isn't it? But I bet you don't know what it's for.   (Reaction.)   Yes, to sing! Goodness you're bright! Right then, as loud as you can to wake them up. Away you go -

(Allows Audience to sing a few bars, then lets them peter out.)

I said away you go and it sounds as if you've gone altogether. Let's try again. Ready?   (Reaction.)

HUMPTY DUMPTY

I said, READY? (Reaction.) That's the spirit!

(Audience sings number.)

Yes, that was very good - for a lullaby. But we want to wake them up. So, once more -

(Audience sings again. KING and RANK begin to stir.)

Well done!

RANK	Was that reveille?
KING	Ooh, I wish I could remember to order a softer bed.
RANK	(suddenly awaking fully) Sir! The Princess, sir!
KING	Good gracious, yes!

(They rise. ROMANO runs on L.)

ROMANO	So, this is the way down. I should have known I couldn't trust Fowlpest. But what was all that singing?
HETTY	Well, they'd been bewitched so my friends here helped me to wake them up.
RANK	(dragging FILE up) File, on your feet!
FILE	(with eyes still closed) Yes, off to bye-byes. Come on, teddy bear.

(Picks RANK up.)

RANK	Leggo!
ROMANO	He still seems a bit dozy. Can I make a suggestion?
HETTY	Any time, dear!
ROMANO	Perhaps you should get some of the children to sing a bit closer to him.
HETTY	You don't mean up here?

(ROMANO nods.)

What an original mind you have!

(HOUSELIGHTS UP.)

	Would you do that, boys and girls? I rather think they would.
	(Ad lib while ROMANO, KING and RANK help children onto stage. HETTY puts FILE in C. and groups the children either side of him, then gets them to sing, first in unison, then in competition. FILE increases in wakefulness as they do so.)
FILE	I'm awake! I'm ever so awake! I've never been so awake!
HETTY	Good, then you can tell us which lot sang the best.
FILE	(crossing his arms to point both ways) That lot.
HETTY	A very popular decision. (To Children.) Thank you very much, dears. And just to make sure you get back to the right mummies and daddies, we'll make them sing to guide you.
	(She encourages Audience to sing as KING, ROMANO, RANK and FILE help children down. HOUSELIGHTS OUT. ILLUMINATED SIGN starts flashing.)
ROMANO	Look! It's telling us it's time we went.
HETTY	(to Audience) You can sing us on our way then. And as it's the last time, raise the roof -
	(Audience sing. Fly SONG SHEET as they do so. HETTY, etc. exit into cleft.
	<u>MUSIC 62</u>
	BLACKOUT. Fly cloth.)

HUMPTY DUMPTY

Scene Ten : Goblin Land

Fullset. A subterranean cavern. Cut-out rock backing in front of the cyclorama, which is dimly lit. Rock wings L. and R. Dilapidated old throne R.C. with one arm missing.

The CHORUS are discovered as very aged GOBLINS with UNDERDOWN, their king, the oldest of them all.

MUSIC 63 SUBTERRANEAN WE

UNDERDOWN
We're the people of Downunderere,
The remnants of a yesteryear.
We are older folk than we appear,

ALL
Subterranean we.

UNDERDOWN
In the Iron Age where we have been
On Bronze Age kids we're not too keen.
Our true period is Plasticine,

ALL
Subterranean we.
In our dance interpretations
Do not laugh at our gyrations;
They are merely demonstrations
 Of longevity.

UNDERDOWN
Come and visit us and you'll confirm
We're waiting for the end of term.
Please knock loudly and beware of the worm -

ALL
Subterranean we.

(GOBLINS chatter agedly. UNDERDOWN totters to his throne and sits.)

1st GOBLIN
Pray silence for the Monarch of all the Goblins, his Lowness King Underdown of Downunderere.

(GOBLINS cheer shakily.)

UNDERDOWN
Thank you, welcome all you Goblin cobbers to the ten thousandth Annual Goblin Revels. I hope you're all having a ball.

(Various wavery replies of 'Yes' and a quavery 'Whoopee' from one LADY GOBLIN.)

Careful, Maud, remember your palpitations. When

I say our ten thousandth Revels of course, I mean
the ten thousandth since I've been on the throne.
(Leans on the remaining arm. It falls off.)
Darned thing, it looks as if I shan't be on it much
longer, and you can't get the Koolibah wood for 'em
any more. Not that we could afford it anyway, our
financial situation's rather dicey. For a good many
years now we've kept going on the gold eggs I've
conned out of Addlepate by saying I was after his
daughter. 'Course I was only pretending because
you know me and girls nowadays.

(LADY GOBLIN gives high pitched giggle.)

Don't be silly, Maud, that was over two hundred
years ago. Anyway, something's happening up
above in Goldova and I don't think we'll get any more
of their gold eggs. Of course, I could carry out my
threat of sending you up to overrun the country but
I'm not sure you'd manage it. You might over-walk
it, though - given time.

(Cries from CHICKWEED off L.)

Hullo, someone at the refreshments already.

(CHICKWEED enters propelled on by the PRINCESS,
who has a half-nelson on her again. GOBLINS
react with horrified cries of 'Mortals', 'Humans',
'People', etc.)

CHICKWEED	Ooh! Ow! Ouch! Leggo!
UNDERDOWN	Humans! Real live Mortal Humans! Here, who are you Sheilas?
CHICKWEED	I'm Chickweed and she - ow! - she's my prisoner.
UNDERDOWN	You could have fooled me.
PRINCESS	I'm certainly not her prisoner. She's mine. And who are you?
UNDERDOWN	Don't speak to me like that. I'm royal, I am.
PRINCESS	So am I. I'm a Princess.
UNDERDOWN	Then I can huff you. I'm a King. King Underdown of Downunderere.

PRINCESS	Downunderere? I thought you were King of the Goblins. Where's Downunderere?
UNDERDOWN	Here, of course. You're down under, aren't you? And you're here, so you're Downunderere. It's Goblinese for Goblin Land.
CHICKWEED	Excuse me, but would you mind taking my prisoner off me?
UNDERDOWN	Why should I? I don't want her.
CHICKWEED	Yes, you do. She's the Princess Eglantine.
UNDERDOWN	Oh, that Princess. The trouble is she's a young girl - And what would I do with a young girl? I know there was something, but it's too far off to remember now. All I was really after was the gold eggs.
CHICKWEED	Gold Eggs! Take her off my hands and I'll show you where to get half-a-dozen right away.
UNDERDOWN	Now you're talking. (To PRINCESS.) Right, let her go.
PRINCESS	Shan't.
UNDERDOWN	All right. (To GOBLINS.) Seize her! (To PRINCESS.) You've done it now. In about ten minutes they'll be over there and they'll grab you.
PRINCESS	We'll see about that.
	(She releases CHICKWEED and prepares to deal with GOBLINS who are slowly advancing towards her. CHICKWEED immediately runs behind GOBLINS.)
UNDERDOWN	It's all right. She's let her go.
	(GOBLINS stop.)
	Where are the eggs?
CHICKWEED	Over there! (Points to nest-egg.)
UNDERDOWN	You might have said it was a long walk.
	(He totters slowly to the nest-egg. The Audience reaction takes him aback.)
HETTY	(off L.) Coming! Coming!

	(HETTY runs on L. as UNDERDOWN tries to hobble away.)
	Who is it? Well, well, a naughty little hobbling goblin.
PRINCESS	Hetty!
HETTY	Princess! It's all right. You're safe now.
UNDERDOWN	She's not! Not if I can't have those eggs. Besides, it's coming back to me about girls. Grab her.
	(As GOBLINS move in, ROMANO runs on L. with a sword.)
ROMANO	Stay where you are!
	(GOBLINS stop.)
UNDERDOWN	This place is getting overcrowded. I shall unleash my Goblin multitudes on you. You five multitudes, get him!
	(Male GOBLINS draw swords.
	<u>MUSIC 64</u>
	After a short set-to, ROMANO forces them to back off L. UNDERDOWN appears to go into a trance.)
PRINCESS	(advancing on CHICKWEED) That leaves me free to deal with you.
CHICKWEED	Oh, help!
	(She runs off R. chased by PRINCESS.)
HETTY	(notices UNDERDOWN's strange state) Ah, poor old thing, the excitement's been too much for him. Not even the strength left to fall down.
UNDERDOWN	(suddenly becoming animated) Bingo!
HETTY	Ooh!
UNDERDOWN	I've remembered about young girls. You're not exactly young –
HETTY	(bridling) Well!
UNDERDOWN	But you'll do. Come here!
HETTY	Eh? Aaah! Get off! Help!

HUMPTY DUMPTY

(She runs off L. chased by him. CHICKWEED runs on R. followed by the PRINCESS, who chases her round the throne.)

CHICKWEED Oh, dear, what was Mr Fowlpest's foot-binding spell? Oh, yes. (Runs backwards in order to make magic passes at PRINCESS.)
Magic chains your feet entwine
First one foot -

MUSIC 65

(Sting. PRINCESS stops momentarily then continues after CHICKWEED hopping R. on one foot.)

Ooh! And - and -
And I can't remember the rest of the line.

(GOBLINS run on L. panting heavily, retreating from ROMANO.)

GOBLINS We surrender!

ROMANO So much for the Goblin multitudes. Princess!

PRINCESS (stopping) Romano!

ROMANO Now you really are safe.

(FOWLPEST runs on L.)

FOWLPEST Oh, no, she's not!

(Grabs the PRINCESS and drags her to L. She is still forced to hop.)

CHICKWEED Mr Fowlpest! (She starts to creep R. unobtrusively.)

GOBLINS We don't surrender!

(They grab ROMANO, who has his back to them, and drag him off U.L.)

FOWLPEST Aha! (Calling to off L.) Humpty! I've got her! (To PRINCESS.) So, I win - Chickweed!

(She gives a little screech and bolts off R.)

FOWLPEST Confound the girl. I must find out what she thinks

	she's playing at. (To PRINCESS.) Come with me.
	(He moves R. with PRINCESS impeded by her hopping. KING runs on L. and stops when he sees them.)
KING	Stop! Stop, I say! Stop in the name of – er – of me!
	(As they haven't stopped he starts towards them.)
FOWLPEST	Oh, phooey!
	(Makes a motion as if flinging something at KING.
	MUSIC 66
	(Sting. KING is still running but on the spot.)
	(Dragging PRINCESS off R.) Chickweed!
KING	I can't move forward. He's bewitched me! Army! Help!
RANK	(off L.) Coming, sir!
	(RANK and FILE run on holding rifles out with bayonets fixed.
	MUSIC 67
	Sting. Unfortunately they 'pink' the royal behind.)
KING	Waah!
RANK	(also running on the spot) Sorry, sir. But you said to fix bayonets, sir.
KING	Yes, and look where you fixed 'em!
FILE	I say, why are we running but not getting anywhere?
KING	You've run into my spell. Let's try running backwards.
	(They run off backwards L. CHICKWEED runs on R. and hides behind throne. FOWLPEST runs on R. pulling the PRINCESS who is still hopping.)
FOWLPEST	Chickweed! Come back! Come back!
	(They exit L. CHICKWEED comes from behind throne with a sigh of relief and moves to go off L. FOWLPEST and PRINCESS return from L.)

	Aha!
CHICKWEED	Ooh! (Runs off R.)
FOWLPEST	Come on! What's the matter with you?
PRINCESS	It's something your apprentice did.
FOWLPEST	Ah, the foot-binding spell. Soon have that off.

(He holds her foot and starts to 'peel' the spell off like a sock. ROMANO enters L.)

ROMANO	Ah!
FOWLPEST	Aha!

('Throws' spell at the advancing ROMANO.

MUSIC 68

Sting. ROMANO starts hopping.

| FOWLPEST | He-he! |

(He drags the now free running PRINCESS off R. ROMANO hops a few steps after them then tries to kick the spell off. HETTY runs on L.

MUSIC 69

Sting. She starts hopping.)

ROMANO	Sorry! (He runs off R.)
HETTY	Oh dear, I never was any good at hopscotch.

(She starts kicking as UNDERDOWN runs on L. She does an especially big kick.

MUSIC 70

Sting. UNDERDOWN starts hopping.)

Ah!   (She runs off R.)

| UNDERDOWN | Hey! I've been nobbled! |

(He hops off R. Pause. HUMPTY looks on L., cautiously, then enters.

| HUMPTY | Awfully quiet here. I don't think I like it. It's like my bedroon. All sort of spooky and creepy and - |

(His knees start knocking assisted by wood-block

HUMPTY DUMPTY — Sc. 10

noise from DRUMMER.)

What's that noise? Oh, it's me. Stop it! (Holds knees to stop them.) My tummy will start rumbling in a minute. It always does when I get nervous.

(Effect 15. Tummy rumbling.)

There. I must eat something to stop it.

(He takes a magic biscuit and starts to eat. Rumbling dies away as CHICKWEED creeps on backwards from L.)

That's better.

CHICKWEED	(swings round) Humpty! (Starts to back off again.)
HUMPTY	Hullo. (Offering bag.) Have a – (He turns.)

MUSIC 71

(Sting.)

Have a me!

CHICKWEED	What?
HUMPTY	I mean, have me! I want you! I love you!
CHICKWEED	But you love the Princess.
HUMPTY	Not any more.
CHICKWEED	You're only making fun of me.
HUMPTY	I'm not. I just love you.
CHICKWEED	You beast! (Jumping up and down.) You don't! You don't! You don't!
HUMPTY	You beauty! (Jumping up and down.) I do! I do! I do! Oh, Chickweed, I really do.
CHICKWEED	Really?
HUMPTY	Honestly!
CHICKWEED	Truly?
HUMPTY	Truthfully! Marry me, Chickweed.

CHICKWEED	Only if you'll marry me.

MUSIC 72

(They kiss lightly.)

Oh, Humpty!

HUMPTY	Oh, Chickweed!
BOTH	(whirling round) Wheee!

(FILE, RANK and the KING run on backwards from L.)

KING	Have we nearly got anywhere yet?
FILE	I don't know, I can't see where we're going, anyway.

(HETTY runs on backwards from L. and collides with the others. They all collapse in a heap. FOWLPEST, with the PRINCESS, runs on R. with ROMANO not far behind.)

FOWLPEST	Humpty! Quick, give her a biscuit and take her, my boy! She's yours!

(Thrusts PRINCESS at HUMPTY.)

PRINCESS	No!
ROMANO) KING) RANK) FILE) HETTY)	No!!
FOWLPEST	Yes!!!
HUMPTY	NO!
OTHERS	What?!
HUMPTY	I don't want her, I just want Chickweed. I don't even want the crown. (Plonks it on the KING's head.) Here!
KING	Ow! Thank you, but ow! (Rises.)
FOWLPEST	Humpty!
HUMPTY	Anyway, Eglantine loves Romano and he loves her, so I think they should marry.

CHICKWEED) HETTY) RANK) FILE) ROMANO) PRINCESS)	Yes!
KING	NO!
	(General consternation.)
PRINCESS	But, Father –
KING	I'm sorry, my dear, but from what Romano told me about himself you can't marry because –
FOWLPEST	Because they're brother and sister!
	(Even more consternation.)
	I stole away the King's baby son to put my son, Humpty, in his place. And the babe I stole away I left with a band of gipsies, and there he is now, the King's real son –
OTHERS	Romano!
	MUSIC 73
KING	No, not Romano. He's – Little Egbert!
ROMANO	Oh no!
PRINCESS	Oh dear! Are you sure?
FOWLPEST	Sure? I can prove it. The Royal babe had a curious egg-shaped strawberry mark on his –
KING	Stop! How do you know that? Only members of the royal family know of the curious egg-shaped strawberry mark on his –
FOWLPEST	I know because I'm part of the royal family. I'm – (He tears off his moustache.)
KING	Big Egbert!
	MUSIC 74
FOWLPEST	Yes.
KING	My naughty non-identical twin brother whom I named my baby son after and whom I sent into

HUMPTY DUMPTY

	exile because you tried to usurp my throne.
FOWLPEST	Yes, yes! I am your naughty non-identical twin brother whom you named your baby son after and whom you sent into exile because I tried to usurp your throne.
FILE	He is his naughty non-iden –
HETTY	All right, dear. They've got that bit now.
FOWLPEST	Anyway, that's why I took up magic – to get my revenge. And I've succeeded!
ROMANO	No, you haven't. Because I'm not the King's real son. I haven't got a curious egg-shaped strawberry mark on my –
HUMPTY	But I have! I'll show you.
CHICKWEED	(a little worried) Humpty!
HUMPTY	(but he plonks the biscuits in the KING's hands, rolls up his sleeve and we see the mark on his elbow) There!

MUSIC 75

(General gasp of amazement.)

KING	What can this mean?
HETTY	I know! It's my fault! It must have happened when I was a young nursemaid! (Breaks off to address the M.D. confidentially.) This is the bit I told you about at the beginning, dear. Remember? (To FOWLPEST.) Yes, I looked after both the royal babes, yours and His Majesty's. But on the day you tried to usurp the throne, everything was topsy-turvy and somehow the babes crawled into the larder and got at the strawberry jam. They came out covered in strawberry marks all over. I must have mixed 'em up.
ROMANO	Thank goodness! I'm not Little Egbert after all.
HUMPTY	(unhappily) No, but I am.
CHICKWEED	(hugging him) You'll always be Humpty to me.

PRINCESS	And you'll always be Romano to me. We can get married now, can't we, Daddy?
KING	Of course, my dear.
HUMPTY	And Daddy, can we get married too?
KING	Certainly, we'll have a grand double wedding.
ALL	Hurray!
FOWLPEST	Romano? <u>My</u> son? I cast my own son away to a band of gipsies. Oh, magic, where have you misled me? I renounce you - forever!
	(UNDERDOWN hops wearily on from R. HETTY squeals and runs behind KING.)
UNDERDOWN	It's all right, I can't keep up the pace. But it was a nice thought while it lasted. (Sinks onto his throne and drops off to sleep.)
HETTY	What a relief! But I'm still all of a doo-dah.
KING	Never mind, have a biscuit to calm you down.
	(She takes one.)
	I'm in a bit of a dither myself. (He takes a biscuit.)
FOWLPEST	No! (Snatches the bag of biscuits and throws it D.R.) Don't eat!
BOTH	(having taken a bite) Why not, they're -
	(They turn to each other.)
	<u>MUSIC 76</u>
	(Sting.)
	Lovely!
KING	Cancel that grand double wedding. We'll have a grand triple wedding!
HETTY	Oh, Addlepate!
HUMPTY	And to think, none of this would have happened if I hadn't been put in an egg and sat on a wall.

HUMPTY DUMPTY

MUSIC 77 HUMPTY DUMPTY   Glee

(During number they move D. S.)

ALL

Humpty Dumpty sat on a wall,
Humpty Dumpty had a great fall;
All the King's horses and all the King's men
Couldn't put Humpty together again.

Repeat.

Humpty Dumpty, etc.,
Couldn't put Humpty together, together again.

Humpty Dumpty, etc.,
Couldn't put Humpty,
Couldn't put Humpty,
Couldn't put Humpty together again.

(Close traverse tabs.)

Scene Eleven : Sheer Magic

Traverse tabs.

MUSIC 78

ALBUMENIA enters R. with a broomstick, she is humming the 'Wedding March'. (Broomstick has fine nylon line attached. The line goes over a swivel in the flies.)

ALBUMENIA

You see, it worked my drastic action,
And by more than just a fraction.
But Fowlpest giving up his art
Has rather left me in the cart.
For which, I fear, there's but one cure,
My magic too I must abjure.
So broomstick one last sweep around
Lest there's some old spells on the ground.
(She sweeps and discovers biscuits D. R.)

What's this? Some biscuits? How delicious!
They look most wholesome and nutritious.
They'll solace me in this grave hour
In which I now – renounce my power!

(Drum roll, LIGHTS FLICKER, cymbal crash.)

There, it's gone. I couldn't do even a simple card trick now, dears. But I've no regrets. Well, just one. I do wish I'd learnt to make my broomstick fly.

(Swanee whistle. Broomstick rises from her hand and disappears. She watches it astonished and follows its course as it apparently traverses overhead and descends on the other side with a thump. Effect 16.)

FOWLPEST   (off L.)   Ow!

ALBUMENIA   Oh dear!

(FOWLPEST enters L. rubbing his head.)

FOWLPEST   That's it, hit a man when he's down. Typical of you, Albumenia. No sense of fair play –

ALBUMENIA   But –

FOWLPEST   No restraint –

ALBUMENIA   But I –

FOWLPEST   No tact –

ALBUMENIA   But I'm trying –

FOWLPEST   I know you are. You can't even let me talk without interrupting.

ALBUMENIA   I'm trying to apologise, you silly man. Look, have a biscuit.

FOWLPEST   Certainly not. You'll have put something in it.

ALBUMENIA   I haven't. I'll show you.   (Takes one and bites.) See? Quite harmless.

FOWLPEST   (grudgingly takes one)   Well –

ALBUMENIA   Such foolishness. Yes, I'm afraid, Fowlpest, you really are –

HUMPTY DUMPTY

(Turns to look at him.

MUSIC 79

Sting.)

So wise! In fact, to wax a little lyrical -
'Thou art as wise as thou art beautiful'.

FOWLPEST   Yes, yes, that's very true. I am.   (Bites biscuit.)   But I'm afraid that you, Albumenia, you -

(Turns to look at her.

MUSIC 80

Sting.)

Oh Albumenia baby! You really take the biscuit!

MUSIC 81   I NEVER THOUGHT

FOWLPEST
I never thought
That so homely an exterior
Could turn into a personable person.

ALBUMENIA
I never thought
That a creature so inferior
Could prove to be a better, not a worse 'un.

FOWLPEST
Though you have made me mad with frustration
I'm quite prepared to give you probation.

ALBUMENIA
Though I have longed to donk you one in the eye
Why, I'll give it a try.
I always thought
You're a really lousy actor
And each little lie you told would be a big 'un.

FOWLPEST
I always thought
You'd a face just like a tractor
On a foggy Tuesday afternoon in Wigan.

BOTH
But on maturer consideration
I find I've got a novel sensation -
I never thought that I could fall in love with you,
   You, be-doo-be-doo-doo.

FOWLPEST
I never thought
That a schemer so nefarious

	Could be a girl as innocent as you are.
ALBUMENIA	I never thought That with villainies so various You seem to be angelically pu-ah.
FOWLPEST	Though all my plans have failed in fruition, You've given me another ambition.
ALBUMENIA	Maybe you've got a magic that I don't know So, let's give it a go. I never thought Such an unattractive creature Could lead up to such an interesting sequel.
FOWLPEST	I never thought I'd be very glad to meet yer Not as better, not as worse, but as an equal.
ALBUMENIA	I might consent to dancing with you, sir.
FOWLPEST	That's if it's O.K. with our Producer.
BOTH	I never thought that I could fall in love with you, You, be-doo-be-doo-doo-CHAH!
	(They exit. Open traverse tabs.)

Scene Twelve : The Palace Throne Room

Fullset. A glittering Palace setting. A rostrum in front of the cyclorama, which is colourfully lit. A cut-out balustrade runs along the back of the rostrum. Steps in C. coming down from the rostrum. Palace wings L. and R.

MUSIC 82 CORTEGG Reprise for walk-down.

CHORUS enter in pairs, one from each side of rostrum, take their bow D.C., and back to form diagonal lines L. and R. PRINCIPALS follow similar procedure, forming diagonal lines in front of them. UNDERDOWN enters from L. and backs to L. DOT enters from R. and CARRYONE from L. and both back to R. RANK enters from L. and FILE from R. and both back to L. KING enters from R. and backs to R. CHICKWEED enters from L. and backs to L. ALBUMENIA enters from R. and backs to R. FOWLPEST enters from L. and backs to L. HUMPTY enters from R. and backs to R. HETTY enters from L. and backs to L. <u>Music stops.</u> ALL turn U. S. PRINCESS enters R. on rostrum and ROMANO L.

ALL Hurray!

(PRINCESS and ROMANO move D.C. to take their bow then the PRINCIPALS move into line with them and the CHORUS move U. S. onto rostrum.)

ROMANO Now all there is to tell is told.

HETTY You've look'd after our eggs of gold –

KING Fathers and sons are reunited –

PRINCESS And couples three their troths have plighted.

ALBUMENIA No, couples four, dear, us as well.

FOWLPEST Yes, we're uniting for a spell.

(HORSES neigh.)

FILE I think they mean it's couples five

(HORSES nod.)

ROMANO But more than that we can't contrive.

HUMPTY So now that we'll all live in clover,
Our story of an egg is – '<u>ova</u>'!

ALL Ooh!

<u>MUSIC 83</u> ANY EXCUSE FOR A PARTY (reprise 18)

TUTTI Today it is somebody's birthday,
 Somebody's passed an exam.
Someone we know's getting married
 And somebody's buying a pram;
We've had a wonderful party,

We have been having a ball,
And now that the party is over
  We are saying goodnight to you all.
You kept festivities humming,
Thank you sincerely for coming,
And now that the party is over
We're saying, we're saying, we're saying goodnight
                      to you all.

CURTAIN

FURNITURE AND PROPERTY PLOT

PART ONE Scene 1

Set Onstage

U.C. Egg on wall (See 'Special Instructions')
L. Trick tub table outside Inn (trap door in top which is opened to feed articles into HETTY's basket)
2 Rifles (2 of CHORUS)

Off R.

Mirror in wings to guide (FILE)
Trick rifle (fitted with device to release a small flag with 'BANG' on it to hang down from the muzzle) (FILE)
Trick shopping basket, very small, (it has no base) containing a spare shopping bag (HETTY)
White broomstick with 'L' plates (ALBUMENIA)
Box Black Magic chocolates (ALBUMENIA)
Signs: 'I AM OUT', 'YES', 'LOOK AT THE WALL' (to be pushed from ALBUMENIA's house)
Ticker tape (to be fed through letter box)
Box Milk Tray chocolates (to be handed on)

Off L.

Imposing letter (KING)
2 Saddles (RANK & FILE)
Trick bouquet (FOWLPEST)
2 Nylon lines fitted with small 'crocodile' clips (to be fitted to CHICKWEED's hat and CHICKWEED's cloak)

Set behind Inn:

Packet of tea
Jar of coffee
Tin of cocoa
Packet of sugar
Bag of liquorice allsorts
Bag of jelly babies
Bag of wine gums
Bag of Guinness gums
Bunch of carrots
3 Bunches of radishes
Long French loaf
Yard of tripe (piece of flannel)
Long string of sausages
Packet of spaghetti
Large wooden knitting needles
Double toilet roll
Nest egg containing a dozen gold eggs (6 should be easily detachable)
(to be fed up through tub table)

Off as convenient

2 Rifles (2 of CHORUS)
Pieces of broken egg shell (to be put on in Blackout)

Personal

Swagger stick (RANK)
Crown (KING)
Spur fitted on L. slipper (KING)

Scene 2

Off L.

Rubber ball with silver glitter on it (FOWLPEST)
Fishing rod (without line) (to be handed on)
Magic wand (CHICKWEED)

Off R.

Rubber ball with blue glitter on it (ALBUMENIA)

Scene 3

Set Onstage

3 Nosebags (beside each horse stall)
Bridle (on floor)
Broom (FILE)

Off R.

Birthday cake on a plate (piece of cake cut out, small file set in it) (PRINCESS)
Christmas pudding (a flattened disc with a sprig of holly on it) (HUMPTY – for use in Sc. 4)
Large shopping bag, containing vinegar bottle and very large sheet of brown paper) (HETTY)

Off L.

Pieces of broken egg shell (RANK & FILE)
Large glue-pot and brush, (glue-pot filled with foamed up shaving soap coloured brown) (RANK)
Small Gripfix tub and applicator (tub filled with foamed-up shaving soap) (FILE)

Scene 4

Off R.

Slapstick bat (HARLEQUIN)

Off L.

Crumbled pieces of polystyrene (to be thrown on if Snow Lantern is not used)
Rice grains (to be thrown on if Rain Lantern is not used)

Scene 5

Off R.

Broomstick (ALBUMENIA)

Off L.

Blue glitter ball (FOWLPEST)
Second blue glitter ball (HETTY)

Off as convenient

Ermine tipped robe)
Ring)
Orb) (CHORUS)
Sceptre)
Throne)

PART TWO Scene 6

Set Onstage

Cauldron and fire (U.C.)
Treestump (D.R.)

Off R.

Castanets (KING)
Gipsy headscarf (FOWLPEST)
Trick card (see 'Special Instructions') (FOWLPEST)

Off L.

Castanets (HETTY)
Round disc inscribed 'SPLLE' (FOWLPEST)
Round disc inscribed 'SPELL' (FOWLPEST)
2 Daggers (2 of CHORUS)
Hat with four folded paper strips each marked with a cross (KING)
Sheet (KING)
Sheet (HETTY)
Sheet (RANK)
Sheet (FILE)
2 Folded sheets (DOT & CARRY-ONE)

Sheet (ROMANO)
Tray with 10 mugs)
(1 of CHORUS)

Scene 7

Off R.

Broomstick with crumpled handle (ALBUMENIA)
Piece of paper and quill pen (ALBUMENIA)

Scene 8

Set Onstage

Double bed with bedclothes (U.C.)
Table with nylon lines attached to pull it to L. (L. of bed)
Chest with hinged lid, long enough for a person to lie full length (at foot of bed)

Off R.

Candlestick with lighted candle (HUMPTY)
Plate with huge prop sandwich (HUMPTY)
Crown (HUMPTY)
Nylon line (to attach to door to pull it shut)
Canes (to push open windows)
Prop skeleton, suspended from a stick (pushed through windows and jiggled to make it dance)
Ghost sheet (KING)
Ghost sheet (RANK
Chost sheet (FILE
Blunderbuss (HUMPTY)
Oil can (FOWLPEST)
Letter (GIPSY GIRL - CHORUS)

Off L.

Ball and chain and head with movable mouth like a ventriloquist's doll (1 of CHORUS)

Lighted taper (FOWLPEST)
Ghost sheet (HETTY)
Ghost sheet (ROMANO)
Powder horn and leather shot pouch (KING)
2 Ghost sheets (DOT & CARRYONE)

Off C.

Blowpipe (to push through flap and blow out candle)
Starter's pistol (to be fired off, Effect 14)

Scene 9

Off R.

Broomstick (ALBUMENIA)
Bag of magic biscuits (FOWLPEST)
Miner's helmet with Davy lamp (HETTY)
Coalscuttle (HETTY)

Scene 10

Set Onstage

Dilapidated throne with only one arm - the armrest should be just balanced in place (R.C.)
5 Short swords (GOBLINS - CHORUS)

Off L.

Sword (ROMANO)
2 Rifles with bayonets attached (RANK & FILE)
Magic biscuit bag (HUMPTY)

Scene 11

Off R.

Broomstick (nylon line going over a swivel in flies attached to it) (ALBUMENIA)

SPECIAL INSTRUCTIONS

<u>Scene 1</u>

Egg on wall
: The cut-out egg is placed thick end downwards on the back of the wall. It is attached to a round block of wood extending below the base of the egg and resting on a ledge set below the top of the wall on its concealed side. Extending downwards from the wood block in an inverted 'V' shape are two wooden arms, which are operated to make the egg rock.

Smoke puffs
: The puffs are pads of cotton wool fitted at intervals on a nylon line. One end of the line goes over a swivel in the flies and is pulled over this to make the smoke rise.

<u>Scene 6</u>

Trick card
: A thick card about 6" x 8" has a flap 3" x 8" hinged horizontally across the centre. Fowlpest displays the card holding the flap up with his thumb to cover the upper half of the card and showing the three crosses marked on it. As he passes his other hand across the card he releases the flap with his thumb so that it falls over the lower half of the card and the crosses have apparently disappeared.

<u>Scene 8</u>

Ancestral portrait
: The eyes are painted on discs superimposed on the picture attached by nails to wooden blocks on the reverse side and which are turned to make the eyes swivel.

Ghostly figure
: A trick costume with a framework of false shoulders that rest on the wearer's head topped by a ruff.

Ship picture
: The top half of the picture is sky and the bottom half sea, but set about $\frac{1}{2}$ in. in front. Into the slot thus made the sailing ship is fitted. It is constructed in two pieces joined by a split pin and fine thread lines are attached to the end of each piece. A tube from a powder puffer is inserted in a hole above the split pin. When the

blunderbuss is fired a puff is given from the powder puffer and the tube is quickly pulled out. The thread lines are operated to pull up the two sections of the ship and then the whole ship is slowly pulled out of sight.

EFFECTS PLOT

PART ONE Scene 1

1. Deep church bell   Tape or grams.

Scene 4

2. Thunder roll   Tape, grams or thunder sheet.

PART TWO Scene 8

3. Cackling laugh   Tape or stage mike, R. speaker.
4. Squeak of door handle   Tape, R. speaker or spot effect R.
5. Creak of door   Tape, R. speaker or spot effect R.
6. Ghastly groan   Tape or stage mike, L. speaker.
7. Clank of ball and chain Tape, L. speaker or spot effect L.
8. Ghastly groan   Tape or stage mike, L. speaker.
9. Wind noise   Tape or grams R. speaker, or wind machine off R.
10. Rattling bones   Tape, R. speaker, or spot effect R.
11. Squeak of door handle Tape, R. speaker, or spot effect R.
12. Creak of door   Tape, R. speaker, or spot effect R.
13. Rattling bones   Tape, R. speaker, or spot effect R.
14. Starter pistol   Off U.C.

Scene 10

15. Tummy rumbling   Tape.

Scene 11

16. Thump of broomstick
    falling   Off L.

MUSIC PLOT

PART ONE

1. Ovature   Orchestra

Scene 1

2. DOING IT ON THE CHEEP   CHORUS

3.	RANK's entrance music	Orchestra
4.	FILE's entrance music, reprise 3	Orchestra
5.	PRINCESS's entrance music.	Orchestra
6.	MONOTONOUS	PRINCESS
7.	KING's entrance fanfare	Orchestra
8.	THE WHOLE STORY IN AN EGGSHELL	KING and PRINCESS
9.	DOT & CARRYONE's entrance music	Orchestra
10.	HETTY's entrance music	Orchestra
11.	TOP OF THE WORLD	HETTY
12.	ROMANO's entrance music	Orchestra
13.	SO CAN I	ROMANO
14.	SWEET NOTHING	PRINCESS & ROMANO
15.	ALBUMENIA's entrance music	Orchestra
16.	FOWLPEST's entrance music	Orchestra
17.	Egg falling music	Orchestra
18.	ANY EXCUSE FOR A PARTY	HUMPTY & Ensemble
19.	ALBUMENIA's music, reprise 15. (Continue to end of scene and as link to Scene 2.)	Orchestra

Scene 2

20.	Music sting	Orchestra
21.	Wish music	Orchestra
22.	Sting, reprise 20	Orchestra
23.	Wish, reprise 21	Orchestra
24.	BONK! (Continue, orchestra only, as link to next scene and segue into reprise of 3.)	FOWLPEST & CHICKWEED

Scene 3

25.	PLAY WITH ABANDON	KING, HETTY, HUMPTY, RANK & FILE

Scene 4

26.	IT MUST BE LOVE	HUMPTY & CHICKWEED
27.	JINGLE BELLS	Orchestra
28.	Intro for ballet	Orchestra

Scene 5

28.	(contd.) SPECTRUM BALLET	CHORUS
29.	ALBUMENIA's music, reprise 15	Orchestra
30.	HARLEQUIN transferring crown, reprise 28, intro only	Orchestra

31.	CORTEGG	CHORUS
32.	Hentr'acte, reprise 31	Orchestra

PART TWO

Scene 6

33.	EGGUIDILLAS	CHORUS, KING, HETTY, DOT & CARRYONE
34.	RANK & FILE spy music	Orchestra
35.	CHICKWEED's creeping music	Orchestra
36.	CHICKWEED creeping, reprise 35	Orchestra
37.	Haunting music	Orchestra
38.	Sting, reprise 20	Orchestra
39.	STARS IN YOUR EYES	ROMANO, PRINCESS & CHORUS
40.	Sting, reprise 20	Orchestra
41.	Reprise 24 for scene link and -	Orchestra

Scene 7

42.	- segue into reprise of 15	Orchestra
43.	Balloon music	Orchestra
44.	Sting, reprise 20	Orchestra
45.	Sting, reprise 20	Orchestra
46.	Sting, reprise 20	Orchestra
47.	Haunting music, reprise 37 for scene link	Orchestra

Scene 8

48.	Haunting music, reprise 37	Orchestra
49.	Haunting music, reprise 37	Orchestra
50.	Haunting music, reprise 37	Orchestra
51.	Chase music	Orchestra
52.	Chase, reprise 51	Orchestra
53.	Chase, reprise 51	Orchestra
54.	RULE BRITANNIA	Orchestra
55.	Hurry music, link to next scene	Orchestra

Scene 9

56.	Sting and ROMEO & JULIET	Orchestra
57.	ALBUMENIA's music, reprise 15	Orchestra
58.	Sting, reprise 20	Orchestra
59.	Sting, reprise 20	Orchestra
60.	Sting, reprise 20	Orchestra
61.	TOP OF THE WORLD, reprise 11, refrain only	HETTY & AUDIENCE

62. Reprise 11, as link to next scene and segue into 63 — Orchestra

Scene 10

63. SUBTERRANEAN WE — UNDERDOWN & CHORUS
64. Fight music — Orchestra
65. Sting, reprise 20 — Orchestra
66. Sting, reprise 20 — Orchestra
67. Sting, reprise 20 — Orchestra
68. Sting, reprise 20 — Orchestra
69. Sting, reprise 20 — Orchestra
70. Sting, reprise 20 — Orchestra
71. Sting, reprise 20 — Orchestra
72. Kiss, reprise 26 — Orchestra
73. Dramatic chord — Orchestra
74. Dramatic chord, reprise 73 — Orchestra
75. Dramatic chord, reprise 73 — Orchestra
76. Sting, reprise 20 — Orchestra
77. HUMPTY DUMPTY, Glee — Ensemble
78. Reprise 15 as link to next scene — Orchestra

Scene 11

79. Sting, reprise 20 — Orchestra
80. Sting, reprise 20 — Orchestra
81. I NEVER THOUGHT — ALBUMENIA & FOWLPEST

Scene 12

82. CORTEGG, reprise 31 for walk-down — Orchestra
83. ANY EXCUSE FOR A PARTY, reprise 18 — Tutti

www.ingramcontent.com/pod-product-compliance
Ingram Content Group UK Ltd.
Pitfield, Milton Keynes, MK11 3LW, UK
UKHW021843210426
5322IPUK00022B/433